MEDIEVAL IRI

witl

THE IRISH BARDIC POET

JAMES CARNEY

MEDIEVAL IRISH LYRICS
Selected and translated

with

THE IRISH BARDIC POET
*A study in the relationship
of Poet and Patron*

THE DOLMEN PRESS

Set in Pilgrim type and assembled by Redsetter Limited, Dublin.
Printed in Ireland by —
O'Brien Promotions Ltd.
for the publishers.

The Dolmen Press Limited
Mountrath Portlaoise Ireland

Designed by Liam Miller

Medieval Irish Lyrics and *The Irish Bardic Poet*
first published separately, 1967
New edition in one volume, 1985.

ISBN 0 85105 360 2

The Dolmen Press receives financial assistance from
The Arts Council, An Comhairle Ealaíon, Ireland.

CONTENTS

INTRODUCTION

The title of the present work 'Medieval Irish Lyrics' calls
for some explanation, if not indeed for apology. Certain
possible titles—all of which would have been open to
some objection—had been pre-empted: 'Ancient Irish
Poetry' by Kuno Meyer, 'Early Irish Lyrics' by Gerard
Murphy, and 'Early Irish Poetry' by myself. There
remained to me the possibility of calling the present work
'Medieval Irish Lyrics' with the unhappy consciousness
that the term 'medieval' was being somewhat misapplied
to certain poems in the collection. The first difficulty,
of course, is that the book contains Gaelic poems and
poems in Latin written by Irishmen. Every language in
using such terms as 'old,' 'medieval' and 'modern' has its
own internal categorization. In Latin we may correctly re-
gard any poem written, say about 600 A.D., as 'medieval.'
But a poem written in Gaelic at that date, or indeed three
centuries subsequently, would be classed as 'old.' We
may end this apology with a word of direction to the
reader. All the Latin poems printed here are correctly
labelled 'medieval,' having regard to the internal
categorization of Latin. The Gaelic poems which have
been dated in the notes from the seventh to the tenth
century are, in the internal categorization of Irish, 'old'
rather than 'medieval.' Linguistically the medieval period
in Irish ends about 1250 A.D., so there are four poems
which could be classed as 'early modern' (XXXVII, XLI)
or 'modern' (VIII, XL). But for these I feel that less
apology is needed. The division of the Irish language into
'old' (600-900 A.D.), 'medieval' (900-1250 A.D.), 'early
modern' (1250-1700 A.D.) and 'modern' (1700, onwards)

vii

is a purely linguistic classification. The Gaelic language in Ireland remained comparatively untouched by the two great events that ushered in the modern world, the Renaissance and the Reformation. Consequently, from a general European point of view much of the folk material recorded in Ireland in recent decades may properly be regarded as reflecting the medieval rather than the modern world, being medieval in spirit if not in language. Indeed, so traditional are contemporary Irish folk tales that they cling to the notion of a world of three continents so that if one sails far enough into the western ocean one will come, not to America, but to walls of brass which are in fact the horizon.

IRISH METRES

A very few years ago any scholar writing on Irish metres would begin with the statement that the verse forms generally used in Irish in the period 600-900 A.D. derive from an early Irish imitation of the verse forms of Latin hymns. The similarities are that in Irish verse and in Latin hymns there is a division into quatrains, the lines are based upon a syllable count, usually consisting of seven or eight syllables, and use is made of rhyme. The following quatrain may be quoted as an example of the metre of a Latin hymn; it is from a poem to the Virgin Mary, written in the eighth century by an Irish monk called Cú Cuimne:

> Cantemus in omni die
> concinentes varie
> conclamantes Deo dignum
> ymnum sanctae Marie

The metre of this poem is virtually identical with an Irish metre called *sétna mór*. The syllable pattern is $8^2 + 7^3$ $+ 8^2 + 7^3$, using the formula with which it is usual to describe Irish metres;[1] *varie* rhymes with *Marie*, and, whether intentional or not, there is *deibide* rhyme (about which we will speak below) between *die* and *varie*; there is internal rhyme between *dignum* and *ymnum*. In this verse, of course, the similarities between Latin hymn metres and Irish verse forms are exaggerated. The Irish monk is introducing specific Irish features into the Latin metre known as trochaic tetrameter catalectic of which a pre-Christian example is found in the marching song of Caesar's soldiers:

> Gallias Caesar subègit
> Nicomedes Caesarem.
> Ecce Caesar nunc triùmphat
> qui subegit Gallias.

The syllabic pattern is here also $8^2 + 7^3 + 8^2 + 7^3$, but the typical Irish features of rhyme and internal rhyme are absent.[2]

But the dependence of Irish metres upon Latin hymns has been gravely exaggerated. A brilliant article published in 1963 by Professor Calvert Watkins of Harvard has demonstrated quite clearly that Irish syllabic verse in many of its features is derived from primitive Irish verse forms; he reaches the very important conclusion that 'We

---

1. The large numbers tell the number of syllables in each of the four lines. The superior numbers tell the number of syllables in the last word of the line.
2. In the final words the rhythmical pattern is, of course, counted from the accent (*subègit, triùmphat*).

can now add Irish to the list of languages, Greek, Vedic, and Slavic, which have preserved the metrical form of Indo-European poetry.[3]

Irish metrics is a wide and complicated subject. Here we can hope to do no more than to make a few comments which will, it is hoped, give the reader some appreciation of the technicalities of the Irish verse-forms in the present volume.[4]

Rhyme became an essential part of Irish verse, but it is not part of its ancient Indo-European inheritance. The following archaic poem, which is in a metre of obscure structure, and not apparently syllabic, shows an early tentative experiment with rhyme:

> Ind ráith i comair in dairfedo,
> ba Bruidgi, ba Cathail,
> ba Aedo, ba Ailello,
> ba Conaing, ba Cuilíni,
> ocus ba Máele Dúin.
> Ind ráith d'éis cach ríg ar úair,
> ocus int slúaig, foait i n-úir.[5]

---

3. *Celtica* VI, 249.
4. The reader is referred to Gerard Murphy, *Early Irish Metrics*, Dublin, 1961; Eleanor Knott on Irish Classical Poetry (In *Early Irish Literature*, Eleanor Knott, Gerard Murphy, Introduction by James Carney, Routledge and Kegan Paul, London, 1965, pp. 21-92). These works are to be read in the light of the article by Professor Watkins referred to above.
5. The rhyme is, of course, between *Dúin* and *úir*. The text of the poem is substantially as given by Murphy, *Early Irish Lyrics*, p. xvi.

'The fort beside the oak-grove
was Bruidge's, was Cathal's,
was Conaing's, was Cuilíne's
and it was Máel Dúin's.
One by one, the kings sleep in the earth
and the fort still endures.'

Speaking of the beginnings of rhyme, we may quote the words of Professor Francis Byrne: 'The origins of rhyme are very obscure: it is found neither in the archaic alliterative verse of the Irish and Germanic peoples nor in classical Greek and Latin poetry. It does however appear in the rhetorical prose of the late empire—in the *Golden Ass* of Apuleius as well as in the sermons of St. Augustine. A primitive form occurs in some of the fifth century hymns. But it is in Ireland that is seems to have been developed to its fullest extent both in Latin and in the vernacular.[6]

Any reader, looking through the present collection, will immediately see that Irish rhyme is not the same as the rhyme used in English and in other languages. In fact, what in English would be regarded as full rhyme, in Irish would often be felt as a breach of good style. In Irish rhyme the vowels, generally speaking, must be identical, and the rhyming consonants must be of the same quality, that is, broad or slender.[7] Furthermore, the Irish divided

---

6. 'Latin Poetry in Ireland' by Francis Byrne (in *Early Irish Poetry*, ed. James Carney, Mercier Press, 4 Bridge St., Cork, Ireland).

7. A broad consonant is a consonant preceded by *a, o,* or *u;* a slender consonant is a consonant preceded by *e,* or *i.* However, since Old and Middle Irish orthography is imprecise in this matter the reader without training

the consonants into six classes, and consonants, when single, rhyme only with others from the same class. The following are the classes:

I. Voiced stops: b, d, g. In these poems, in internal or final position, generally represented by p, t, c.

II. Voiceless stops: p, t, c; frequently, in internal or final position, represented by pp, tt, cc.

III. Voiceless spirants: ph (f), th, ch.

IV. Voiced spirants and weakly pronounced voiced liquids (in internal or final position): b (=v), m (=nasal v), d (=th, as in English 'then'), g (as in German 'morgen'), l, n, r.

V. Strongly pronounced voiced liquids: m (=mm, often so written), ll, nn, ng, rr. Consonants of this class, following a long vowel or diphthong, may rhyme with those of class IV.

VI. The consonant s (frequently written ss) rhymes only with itself.

The most characteristic Irish metre is called *deibide* (written *deibhidhe* in modern Irish, and pronounced *devee*). It may be useful for the reader to give a metrical analysis of a single verse (VII, p. 14):

> Sainemlu cech dóen a chruth,
> brestu cech sóer a balcbruth,
> gaíthiu cech bruinniu fo nim,
> fíriánu cech breithemain.

---

will not always recognise the quality of an Irish consonant. For instance, in modern Irish the word for woman is written *bean*, in Old Irish *ben:* in each case the quality of the final consonant is broad. In earlier Irish *bein* is written, when the final consonant is slender.

xii

In this stanza there are seven syllables in each line: *chruth* rhymes with *balcbruth*, the final consonants being identical, from class III above; *nim* rhymes with *breithemain* (which could have been spelt *breithemin*). In Irish the accent normally falls heavily on the first syllable of a word. Hence, in this particular metre, rhyme is between a stressed (*chruth*) and an unstressed syllable (*-bruth*). The internal rhyme between *dóen* and *sóer* in the first couplet may be accidental.

This metre has many variations, one of which, for instance, is to have only three syllables in the first line (as in the third and fourth quatrains on page 34).

We may analyse another quatrain (XV, p. 30):

> Ó do-éctar mo láma
> ot é cnámacha cáela,
> nítat fíu turcbáil taccu
> súas tar na maccu cáema.

This quatrain is in a metre called *rannaigecht bec*. There are seven syllables in each line, and the endings are disyllabic, all of which can be expressed in the formula $7^2 + 7^2 + 7^2 + 7^2$. *cáela* rhymes with *cáema*, having an identical diphthong áe,[8] and *l* and *m* (=nazalized *v*) coming from the same consonantal class. *láma* is metrically related to *cáela* and *cáema* by a device called consonance, which is really a more subtle form of rhyme: it has all the requirements of rhyme, except that the accented vowel element need not be identical, but corresponds only in length: the *m* is from the same

8. This diphthong, expressed in later orthography by *ao*, is followed by a broad consonant.

consonantal class, is broad in quality, and the long vowel *á* balances the diphthong *áe*. There is internal rhyme between *taccu* and *maccu*. It is to be noted that of the twenty-eight syllables in the quatrain ten of them are controlled by the rhyming system.

A poem is not necessarily composed in stanzas of the same metre, and in the poem from which the above quatrain is taken there is considerable variation.

All except three of the Irish poems in the present collection are based on a count of syllables. The two modern poems VIII and XL are in stressed metres which, after an underground existence of some centuries, supplanted syllabic versification in the seventeenth century; poem XXXVIII is a passage from a saga, a piece of heightened prose, which I have thought worthy of dividing into lines and presenting as verse. This piece in some ways resembles the kind of poetry that preceded the stanzaic verse which forms the bulk of the present collection.

Poem I is the earliest in this collection, and in the notes I have shown how it was necessary to reconstruct the original from two defective sources: a seventh-century Latin translation and an Irish version from a late ninth-century life of St. Patrick. The line *Canfaid míchrabud*, missing in the Irish version, had to be based on the Latin *Incantabit nefas*.[9] There is no doubt about *Canfaid*, and *míchrabud* was a perfect rendering of *nefas* and had the advantage that it alliterated with *méis* in the following line. I felt quite happy about this rendering and regarded

---

9. The form, however, should probably be changed to *cechna*, the older form of the third singular future of *canaid*.

the poem as a piece in an archaic irregular metrical structure. But as the work went through the press I developed some doubts. In the first stanza (if we are justified in dividing the poem into stanzas) each line consists of four syllables and ends in a disyllable ($4^2 + 4^2 + 4^2 + 4^2$). In the second stanza, as the text stands, we have a pattern $5^3 + 8^2 + 8^2 + 4^2$. The word that I have reconstructed from the Latin, *míchrabud*, is odd man out in this arrangement, and consequently falls under grave suspicion. I would suggest here that we must seek further for an Irish word of two syllables that would translate *nefas*. This stanza would then have the metrical form $4^2 + 8^2 + 8^2 + 4^2$, and we might compare poem XXXVII in a well-known and popular metre based on the alternation of four and eight syllables.

THE LATIN POEMS[10]

It will be useful to deal first with the Latin poems. II and III are included in some notes written in Latin by Bishop Tírechán towards the end of the seventh century. This bishop could hardly write a sentence in Latin without allowing his native Gaelic idiom to show through, so we may reasonably conclude that these poems must have existed before his time. I have dated them to about 600 A.D., perhaps a little earlier, about which time the first efforts were being made to present material relative to the life of St. Patrick, who had died in 493.[11] III, St.

---

10. References to sources and to earlier discussions of particular poems will be found in the notes.
11. *The Problem of St. Patrick*, James Carney, Dublin, 1961, pp. 131-4.

Patrick's Creed, purports to be the saint's own work—I will leave it to those better versed in St. Patrick's curious Latinity to say whether or not this could be so. But if it is not so, it could be an early versification of a creed which Patrick taught during his mission to the Irish.

St. Columbanus, author of IV (not to be confused with his contemporary, St. Columcille), is one of the earliest of the Irish Latinists whose work has survived in any quantity. He came to the Continent from Ireland about 591. He lived at first in Merovingian Gaul, busied himself with religion, poetry and politics, with the latter so indiscreetly that he had perforce to move to northern Italy. Here, in the land of his second exile, he founded under an Irish rule the monastery of Bobbio, which came to be his most famous foundation. The poem which I translate has been frequently regarded as a boat-song. It is rather, I think, a poetic exhortation to his monks to persevere to the end, with an image drawn from the boat, that by the effort of its crew passes through storm and tempest to the ultimate security of port.

Sedulius Scottus (author of XIX-XXIV) at Christmas about the year 845 arrived on the Continent from Ireland and sought out Hartgar, bishop of Liège. Sedulius has left a great collection of his Latin verse. Those selected for translation here show his career from the day of his arrival until about thirteen years later when, we may presume, he either died or returned to Ireland. He was immediately put in charge of the cathedral school by Hartgar, and we shortly find four other Irishmen employed there. These, who probably include his two initial companions, Sedulius calls 'four charioteers of the Lord, lights of the Irish race.' All through his poems he emphasizes his nationality, and demands that as one who has suffered exile from his own country he be given nothing but the best.[12] Hence his demands for a good table (XXI) and a house safe from robbers and decorated in the most modern style (XX).

In Sedulius's verse we get a very good idea of his conception of the world. It was bounded by India on one side, by Ireland on the other. He was conscious of the Slavs and the Scythians at the extremities of Europe and the margins of Asia, of the Holy Land, Aethiopia, Libya, and the whole ancient world dominated by Romans, Greeks and Hebrews. His immediate world is Italy, especially Rome, and western Europe inhabited by Germans, Franks and Irish. He sees this group being menaced on the south by the Moors and Saracens, and on the opposite side by the heathen Northmen. Poem XXII is a hymn of thanks for a victory gained by Hartgar over the latter—we can compare poem X, written in Irish at the same period and expressing fear of the same enemy.

XXIII is an extract from a much longer poem. Hartgar had promised Sedulius a present of a ram. But before the beast was transferred from the episcopal to the scholastic field, a thief entered the palace grounds. Dogs were set on him—the thief escaped, but the dogs killed the ram.

Sedulius made a long mock-heroic poem about the death of this innocent beast. In what now might seem somewhat dubious taste, he makes a comparison between Christ, the Lamb of God, and the slain ram. Christ died

---

12. The theme of exile is a constant one in Irish poetry from the earliest period. Typical is XXXV, a dramatic poem, put in the mouth of Colum Cille.

for sinners, the innocent ram died for the thief. The lines translated here are indirectly autobiographical, for Sedulius praises the ram for the lack of those very faults which he knew to be conspicuously his own, loquaciousness, love of meat, drink and high society.

These poems of Sedulius, light and personal, give no adequate idea of his accomplishment. He was a social personality, the friend of emperors and high ecclesiastics. But he had gained his position in society by sound and solid scholastic work. He busied himself with Latin grammar and wrote commentaries on the grammatical works of Eutyches and Priscian. He composed a commentary on the gospel of Matthew and another on the epistles of St. Paul. Amongst the works which he had brought from Ireland was a copy of a text called *Proverbia Graecorum* which appears to have been written in Ireland as early as the sixth century.

His most original work was *De Rectoribus Christianis* 'Concerning Christian Rulers,' a treatise on the duties of a prince. This was written for Lothar II, son to the emperor Lothar I. It deals partly with the problem of relations between Church and State, and is regarded as an important contribution to the development of political thought in the Middle Ages. The work is written in prose, but every section is recapitulated in verse. This form of writing was to become increasingly popular in Irish, but we cannot maintain that Sedulius was here following Irish models; he is imitating the form of *De Consolatione Philosophiae* by Boethius.

In form the Latin poems of Sedulius are Carolingian verse of a very high order of competence. Whether or not it will eventually emerge that there is in it any significant

Gaelic element I cannot say. In his poem on the defeat of the Northmen Sedulius reckons the numbers of the slain. He says (as I translate him): 'Count not unknown, count not the menials, on that dread field lay bloody there three times ten thousand.' This, of course, must be ridiculous exaggeration, and as such quite Irish. Typical, however, of the Irish aristocratic attitude to battles is to reckon the numbers of people of some quality who fell, and to dismiss the *daescurshluag* or 'rabble' losses as something of no account.

It is, I would say, almost certain that Sedulius would have written verse in Irish as well as in Latin. There is in the Royal Library of Dresden a Greek text of the thirteen epistles of St. Paul with a Latin interlinear version. The manuscript belongs to the circle of Sedulius. It reflects one of Sedulius's own particular interests, the epistles of St. Paul; the writer knew Greek, as did Sedulius, and amongst other marginalia it contains the names of Hartgar, and of Gunthar, bishop of Cologne, to both of whom Sedulius had written poems. The great medievalist Traube had little hesitation in attributing this manuscript to Sedulius himself. As marginalia in this manuscript there are some quatrains in Irish, including the clever and slightly cynical comment on pilgrimages to Rome which is poem XXXII in the present collection. This quatrain may very well have been composed by Sedulius; it has the epigrammatic quality one would expect from him.

Like any other intelligent man, despite some superficial appearances to the contrary, Sedulius was essentially humble. He could boldly declare his talents, but see their insignificance in universal terms. It is a sign of his humility that, loquacious as he was, he could still sum up a life rich in achievement in the six lines of verse that constitute poem XXIV.

In the introduction to *Ancient Irish Poetry* Kuno Meyer has written: 'In Nature Poetry the Gaelic muse may vie with that of any other nation. Indeed, these poems occupy a unique position in the literature of the world. To seek out and watch and love Nature, in its tiniest phenomena as in its grandest, was given to no people so early and so fully as to the Celt. Many hundreds of Gaelic and Welsh poems testify to this fact. It is a characteristic of these poems that in none of them do we get an elaborate or sustained description of any scene or scenery, but rather a succession of pictures and images, which the poet, like an impressionist, calls up before us by light and skilful touches. Like the Japanese, the Celts were always quick to take an artistic hint; they avoid the obvious and the commonplace; the half-said thing to them is dearest.'

There are a number of poems here that illustrate Meyer's statement, VI, XI, XVI, XXVII, XXXIV. Indeed, poem XVI resembles somewhat the Japanese *haiku*. A poem, similar in metre and spirit, inadvertently omitted from the collection, may be given here:

Int én bec	The little bird
ro léic feit	has whistled
do rind guip	from point of beak
glanbuide;	bright yellow;
fo-ceird faíd	sends a cry
os Loch Laíg	over Loch Laíg

| lon do chraíb | blackbird from branch |
| chrannmuige.[13] | in wooded plain. |

These poems emerge from a Christian society that, at its height, was perhaps the most ascetic that Western Europe has known. The flesh and the Devil were firmly rejected, but the grimness of life was tempered by an acceptance of the beauty of the world, of nature and animal life, as the handicraft of God. There were moments of rebellion when life seemed too hard to bear, and there were doubtless many backsliders. A distinguished Harvard professor has translated the Irish epitaph of the eighth-century monk Cú Cuimne from whose Latin hymn to the Virgin Mary we have already quoted above. I have not seen the translation in print, but simply heard it passed from mouth to mouth and quote it from memory:

> Cú Chuimne in his youth
> read his way through half the truth;
> he let the other half lie
> and gave women a try.
>
> Good for him, in his old age
> he became a full sage;
> he gave women the laugh
> and read the other half.

Sometimes the grim asceticism was relieved by a resort to a wry humour. In a poem written about 1000 A.D. a poet, unfortunately anonymous, puts himself in the dock

---

13. Cf. Murphy, *Early Irish Lyrics*, p. 6.

on a charge of allowing his mind to wander in strange and unseemly places during the singing of the psalms. Indeed, it is possible that the poem formed in his mind during one of the long periods of community prayer, and would thus be part of the substance of his sin:

Is mebul dom imrádud
    a méit élas úaimm
ad-águr a imgábud
    i lló brátha búain . . .[14]

A shame on my thinking
    how it wanders away;
it will cause me embarrassment
    on Last Judgement day.

At psalm time it rushes forth
    on a pathway that's odd,
running, raving, misbehaving
    in the presence of God.

To merry women's company,
    the unvirtuous kind,
through wood and through cities
    faster than the wind.

When road is smooth it travels
    merrily and gay,
but passes just as easily
    the impenetrable way.

14. For the Irish text see Murphy, *Early Irish Lyrics*, p. 38.

It needs no ship to journey
  and the seas go by,
jumps with but a single leap
  from solid earth to sky.

No course of wisdom does it run
  whether near or far
and after all foolishness
  it's back where we are.

Put a fetter on its leg,
  chain it to prayer?
Yes! But in a minute's time
  it's no longer there.

Little use in beating it,
  plying whip or rod:
like an eel's tail it slips away
  from my grasp and from God.

No chain and no dark dungeon
  will hinder its course;
it laughs at seas and fortresses
  is mocking of force.

Dear Christ, lord of chastity,
  chain thinking in place
with power of spirit septiform
  and all His grace.

Make, great elemental God,
  the heart be still,

that you be my only love
and I your will.

May I come to Christ at last
and then to see
that He is no unsteady thing,
not wandering, like me.

Poem XV, which I have called 'Ebbing' is somewhat of a mystery.[15] It has been taken as a dramatic lyric, a presentation in Christian dress of the Hag of Beare, who was in all probability a pagan mythological figure. Before translating this poem I spent some five months reading it with a seminar class, making a fresh examination of the manuscript tradition, and questioning where necessary the hitherto accepted interpretation of phrases, lines and quatrains. The seminar, which was held for one hour weekly, included amongst other distinguished scholars the late Frank O'Connor, the famous Irish short-story writer who was particularly fascinated by this poem. During this study many subtleties and nuances became apparent. The poem is probably ninth century. It is not, in my opinion, a 'dramatic lyric.' When the author says, 'I am the hag of Buí and Beare (*Is mé caillech Bérri Buí*) what is meant is "In my condition, outliving those I love, I resemble the old hag of Beare who lived through seven

---

15. An Irish lyric poem has no title—it is usually quoted by its first line. This poem has been generally known as 'The Lament of the Hag of Beare.' I have deliberately departed from the usual title, which, it seems to me, somewhat prejudices the interpretation.

xxiv

ages." The poem continues as a passionate statement of the poet's own dilemma, having outlived youth and beauty and being mercilessly thrown into an asceticism to which her intellect acceded, but against which every other natural instinct rebelled. Although I say 'her' I am anything but sure that the poem was written by a woman. In an essay on the Irish bardic poet, to be published shortly, I have pointed out how Irish bardic poets, when praising their princely or royal patrons, could assume, through a well-established conceit, the completely feminine role of 'king-lover.' I have written there: 'It could be maintained, but perhaps not with certainty, that one of the finest poems of this type is the ninth-century poem in which the poet speaks in the character of the Old Woman of Beare. The poet, in such an interpretation, was what one may call a "king-lover": when old age was approaching he took unwillingly to religion; he expresses all his past experiences with kings in the person of an old harlot who, after a good spring, summer and autumn, found herself rejected by her patrons in the early months of her winter.'

It may, however, be preferable to take the poem at its face value, that is, as having been written by a woman.[16] There was an Irish queen, Gormlaith, who died in 946.

16. Outside the monastic milieu poetry in Ireland was written largely by hereditary professional poets. Líadan, to whom poem XIII is attributed, is presented in the saga from which the poem is taken, as a professional woman poet. There is also every reason to believe that in the ninth century an educated or aristocratic lady might make a habit of composing verse.

Her father was king of Tara and of Ireland. She married successively three kings, Cerball, king of Leinster, Cormac, king of Munster, and finally Níall Glúndub, king of Ireland. Later she became a figure in romance, giving rise to a tale 'The love of Gormlaith for Níall Glúdub.' Finally in her old age she retired to a convent. Gormlaith can hardly be the writer of this poem: the geographical references suggest strongly that the writer belonged to what is now the county of Tipperary,[17] and it might be difficult, on purely linguistic grounds, to suggest as late a date as 940. But the poem could have been written by an aristocratic woman of somewhat earlier date, whose experiences were somewhat similar to those of Gormlaith. Indeed, with the system of dynastic intermarriage, and the frequent early death of men of the princely warrior caste, the pattern of Gormlaith's marriages would not be unusual. It is doubtful that we shall ever achieve a satisfactory solution of this problem.

I have mentioned above the title of a saga 'The love of Gormlaith for Níall Glúndub.' The very title raises another matter relevant to some of these poems. In early Ireland, in direct contrast to the present age, it may be said that the man and not the woman is the primary love-object. Hence, in early Irish literature, it is more usual to read of the tragic or unrequited love of a woman for a man, rather than the contrary. This is a reflection of life as it was. Irish warrior society, like early Greek society, tended to be male-orientated. Women in sages frequently make

17. Although Gormlaith, as wife of a king of Cashel, knew this area, she could hardly write such a poem without references to Tara or the northern part of Ireland.

their first and natural entry into a love-situation while serving food and drink to the men-folk. Hence we experience the tragedy of love in the suffering of Deirdre and of Gráinne—it is their natural destiny to outlive the warriors they loved. So in poem XII, the wife of Aed mac Ainmirech, king of Tara, remembers him when he is dead. In poem XIII Líadan remembers Cuirithir when he has left her; in XXXVIII we read, in a poetic passage from a saga, of Findabair's passionate remembrance of a single moment in her life when the beauty of her dead lover Fróech was revealed to her.

Most early Irish poetry is anonymous. In the late period that is, from about 1250 onwards, the authorship of a poem is generally stated. To this class belongs XXXVII by Gofraidh Fionn Ó Dálaigh, an excerpt from a longer poem. The poem was written about 1354, and describes, in allegorical terms drawn from Irish mythology, the visit of the poet's patron, Maurice FitzMaurice, to the court of the English king in London.

Poem XXV, two stanzas on India, are an extract from a longer work on world geography—verse was used in Ireland to teach any and every subject. The author, Airbertach mac Cosse, who died towards the close of the tenth century, was *fer léiginn* or chief professor at the monastery of Ros Ailithir (now Ros Carbery in Co. Cork). He was probably the author of Saltair na Rann, the Psalter of Quatrains, a versification of biblical history, one of the most ambitious poems in early Irish.

Máel Ísu Ó Brolcháin, author of XXIX and XXXI, lived throughout the greater part of the eleventh century and died in 1086. Poem XXIX is anonymous in the manuscripts and the reasons for ascribing it to Máel Ísu are discussed elsewhere.[18] The poem at one time gave rise to much comment and theorizing. The name Crínóc is a woman's name, or could be used as such, and means 'Dear little old thing.' Kuno Meyer, who first discovered and published this poem, accepted the poem quite literally, despite difficulties which must be apparent even to a casual reader. He assigned it, on no very good grounds, to the tenth century. Crínóc, he held, was one of those religious women who contracted spiritual marriage (*Geistige Ehe*) with clerics or ascetics of the opposite sex, and he adduced this poem to prove that this custom, suppressed in the Church generally by the council of Nicea in the fourth century, lived on in Ireland until the tenth.

For me the poem always constituted a problem, for Meyer's interpretation, unlikely on the face of it, left too many questions unanswered. But the problem lay upon my mind for many years before the easy and natural solution suggested itself: it was a poem written by a religious in his old age to an old and tattered copy of the Psalms which had been his first lesson book. The solution, which has found general acceptance by scholars, emerged quite clearly when I noted that in early Ireland a boy destined for the Church began his education at the age of seven, and that the Psalter, from which he learned Latin, reading, singing and religion, was his first lesson book. This book, which he had used in his youth in its virgin freshness passed through four generations of young scholars before by some chance it came back into the old priest's hands again.

---

18. See Notes for references.

XVIII, the poem on Fate, is worth some comment. The text was discovered and published by me some twenty-five years ago. It belongs to about the year 900, or perhaps a little later. It is interesting as an exemplification of Irish views on fate and destiny current over a thousand years ago, and, as we shall see, persisting down to modern times. Stanza 6 of this poem, translated quite literally, says: 'It does not stop me from setting out on a journey that someone in a gathering sneezes—the sod on which my tomb-stone has been shaped, I must needs approach it.'

From classical antiquity, down through the middle ages, a sneeze was always considered a bad omen. To avert the evil, in Germany and America, one still says 'Gesundheit'; in Irish one says 'Dia linn,' 'God be with us.' The sod of death idea, however, is so far as I know, confined to Ireland, Iceland and Sweden.[19]

The Irish had a curious belief that for everybody there existed three 'sods' or spots: the 'sod of birth,' the 'sod of death,' and the 'sod of burial.' Each sod was predestined, the sod of burial having its importance in being the pre-destined place of personal resurrection on the Last Day. The sod of death (which may originally have been the same as the sod of burial) came to be thought of in the folk mind as a particular piece of earth somewhere in the world upon which a man one day would tread, and the moment of contact would be that of his death. The

---

19. See an article by Maura Carney, *Arv*, Journal of Scandinavian Folklore, Vol. 13, 1957, pp. 157 ff., Anne Holtsmark, *Lochlann*, Vol. 2, 1962, pp. 122 - 7.

sod seems to beckon each and everyone on, and belief in it still survives in Irish folklore. A common type of folktale tells how a man discovered what was destined to be his sod of death, had it safely, as he thought, disposed of, thrown to the bottom of the sea or otherwise destroyed. But by some wonderful or unexpected circumstance, at the predestined moment, the sod would find its place beneath his feet.

The following is a translation of a passage from a statement written in Irish in 1945 by a 68-year-old Irish-speaker from Doolin, Co. Clare, on the beliefs of the people in his district concerning fate and destiny.

'I wish to mention the belief that the old people had that it was laid out for a person from the time the crown of his head came into the world where his sod of death was. For this person it was laid out that for him, or for her, the side of the road would be as a sod of death, for another the middle of the field, or out on the brown mountain, or in the loneliness of the wood, or—God save us from the danger!—a person could have as sod of death a violent death.

I remember when a poor girl from this town fell down a terrible cliff over there a dozen years ago, what an old neighbour, no longer living for many a day, said. There were droves of people from the towns around present, everywhere taking the full of their eyes fearfully of the poor dead thing who was thrown there on a fissure in the cliff hundreds of feet from the top. This person and that were trying to ease in some way the torment of the girl's father, but what the old man I mentioned had to say when he looked down at the dreadful sight was: " 'Twas her sod of death that was there" *(Sé fód a báis do bhí ann)*.'[20]

We may now make some comment on poem VII which consists of extracts from a much longer poem. Some years ago in the National Library of Ireland I was fortunate enough to come upon twenty-three pages of Irish verse which by a curious mischance had not hitherto come under the notice of scholars. Though the manuscript was seventeenth century, the verse was some nine hundred years earlier; the greater part of it was by a poet who was unknown save for his name: Blathmac son of Cú Brettan son of Congus. Blathmac was of the Fir Rois; in other words he came from an area covering parts of the counties of Louth and Monaghan. His father, who was king of the Fir Rois, had some part in the battle of Allen in 722 and died in 740. His brother Donn Bó died about 759, so we can reasonably date these poems to somewhere in the second half of the eighth century. The discovery of such a significant quantity of early verse illustrates the fact that, owing to the lack of sufficient trained workers in the field, the literature of Ireland in the early centuries is still an incompletely known subject.

Finally it remains to make some comment on the arrangement of these poems. This is only roughly chronological, the chronological factor being frequently ignored in the interests of an interesting juxtaposition. The first poem fittingly introduces Christian Gaelic Ireland and announces the death of paganism. The last, written in the seventeenth century when the Gaelic

---

20. As translated by Maura Carney, loc. cit.

social order had received its death blow, is a somewhat bitter appeal to Irish traditionalist scholars to forget their disputes about the mythical and historical past and by implication to face the hard realities of the present.

As a last word I may point out what by now must be obvious to the reader: many of the poems are poems with which as a scholar I had a particular association. It will not be equally obvious that sometimes a poem was translated because it seemed at one point or another in my life to have relevance to my own experience or feeling.

JAMES CARNEY

Dublin Institute for Advanced Studies
University of California, Los Angeles
December 3rd, 1966.

Acknowledgements

Some of the translations presented here have appeared in other sources: *Ireland Harbinger of the Middle Ages*, Ludwig Bieler, Oxford University Press; *Old Ireland*, ed. Robert McNally S.J., M. H. Gill and Son Ltd., *Studies in Irish Literature and History*, James Carney, Dublin Institute for Advanced Studies; *The Dubliner*, winter 1964 (now *The Dublin Magazine*). For criticism and advice I am indebted to the Rev. Terence McCaughey. My wife also helped with criticism and proof reading.

J.C.

MEDIEVAL IRISH LYRICS

For the memory of my father
PATRICK CARNEY
from Kiltimagh
and of my mother
CONTANCE GRACE
from Thomastown

I

Ticfa Tálcenn

Ticfa Tálcenn
tar muir mercenn,
a thí thollcenn,
a chrann crombcenn.

Canfaid míchrábud
a méis i n-airthiur a thige;
fris-gérat a muinter uile:
'Amén, Amén.'

II

Quis Est Deus?

Quis est Deus
et ubi est Deus
et cuius est Deus
et ubi habitaculum eius?

Si habet filios et filias,
aurum et argentum, Deus vester?

Si vivus semper,
si pulcher,
si filium eius
nutrierunt multi?

2

I

Adze-head

Across the sea will come Adze-head,
crazed in the head,
his cloak with hole for the head,
his stick bent in the head.

He will chant impiety
from a table in the front of his house;
all his people will answer:
'Be it thus. Be it thus.'

II

The Questions Of Ethne Alba

Who is God
and where is God,
of whom is God,
and where His dwelling?

Has He sons and daughters,
gold and silver, this God of yours?

Is He ever-living,
is He beautiful,
was His son
fostered by many?

3

Si filiae eius
carae et pulchrae sunt
hominibus mundi?

Si in caelo
an in terra est?
In aequore,
in fluminibus,
in montanis,
in convallibus?

Dic nobis
notitiam eius:
Quomodo videbitur,
quomodo diligitur,
quomodo invenitur?

Si in iuventute,
si in senectute
invenitur?

III

Deus Noster

Deus noster, Deus omnium hominum,
Deus caeli ac terrae, maris et fluminum,
deus solis ac lunae, omnium siderum,
Deus montium sublimium, valliumque humilium,
Deus super caelo et in caelo et sub caelo.

Are His daughters
dear and beautiful
to the men of the world?

Is He in heaven
or on the earth?
In the sea,
in the rivers,
in the mountains,
in the valleys?

Speak to us
tidings of Him:
How will He be seen,
how is He loved,
how is He found?

Is it in youth
or is it in old age
He is found?

III

St. Patrick's Creed

Our God, God of all men,
God of heaven and earth, sea and rivers,
God of sun and moon, of all the stars,
God of high mountains and of lowly valleys,
God over heaven, and in heaven, and under heaven.

Habet habitaculum
erga caelum et terram et mare
et omnia quae sunt in eis.

Inspirat omnia,
vivificat omnia,
superat omnia,
suffulcit omnia.

Solis lumen inluminat,
lumen noctis et notitias vallat
et fontes fecit in arida terra
et insolas in mari siccas
et stellas in ministerium
maiorum luminum posuit.

Filium habet
coaeternum sibi et consimilem sibi;
non iunior Filius Patri
nec Pater Filio senior.

Et Spiritus Sanctus
inflat in eis;
non separantur Pater
et Filius et Spiritus Sanctus.

He has a dwelling
in heaven and earth and sea
and in all things that are in them.

He inspires all things,
He quickens all things,
He is over all things,
He supports all things.

He makes the light of the sun to shine,
He surrounds the moon and stars,
and He has made wells in the arid earth,
placed dry islands in the sea
and stars for the service
of the greater luminaries.

He has a Son
coeternal with Himself, like to Himself;
not junior is Son to Father,
nor Father senior to the Son.

And the Holy Spirit
breathes in them;
not separate are Father
and Son and Holy Spirit.

IV

En Silvis Caesa

En, silvis caesa fluctu meat acta carina
Bicornis Rheni et pelagus perlabitur uncta.
 Heia viri! nostrum reboans echo sonet heia!

Extollunt venti flatus, nocet horridus imber,
Sed vis apta virum superat sternitque procellam.
 Heia viri! nostrum reboans echo sonet heia!

Nam cedunt nimbi studio, ceditque procella,
cuncta domat nisus, labor improbus omnia vincit.
 Heia viri! nostrum reboans echo sonet heia!

Durate et vosmet rebus servate secundis,
O passi graviora, dabit deus his quoque finem.
 Heia viri! nostrum reboans echo sonet heia!

Sic inimicus agit invisus corda fatigans,
Ac male temptando quatit intima corda furore.
 Vestra, viri, Christum memorans mens personet heia!

State animo fixi, hostisque spernite strofas,
Virtutum vosmet armis defendite rite.
 Vestra, viri, Christum memorans mens personet heia!

IV

Columbanus To His Monks

See, cut in woods, through flood of twin-horned Rhine
passes the keel, and greased slips over seas —
Heave, men! And let resounding echo sound our 'heave'.

The winds raise blasts, wild rain-storms wreak their spite
but ready strength of men subdues it all —
Heave, men! And let resounding echo sound our 'heave'.

Clouds melt away and the harsh tempest stills,
effort tames all, great toil is conqueror —
Heave, men! And let resounding echo sound our 'heave'.

Endure and keep yourselves for happy things;
you suffered worse, and these too God shall end —
Heave, men! And let resounding echo sound our 'heave'.

Thus acts the foul fiend: wearing out the heart
and with temptation shaking inmost parts —
*You men, remember Christ with mind still sounding
'heave'.*

Stand firm in soul and spurn the foul fiend's tricks
and seek defence in virtue's armoury —
*You men, remember Christ with mind still sounding
'heave'.*

Firma fides cuncta superat studiumque beatum,
Hostis et antiquus cedens sua spicula frangit.
Vestra, viri, Christum memorans mens personet heia!

Rex quoque virtutum, rerum fons, summa potestas,
Certanti spondet, vincenti praemia donat.
Vestra, viri, Christum memorans mens personet heia!

V

Is Mebul

Is mebul
élúd Ríg na fírinne
ocus chairte fri demun.

VI

Scél Lemm Dúib

Scél lemm dúib:
dordaid dam,
snigid gaim,
ro-fáith sam;

Firm faith will conquer all and blessed zeal
and the old fiend yielding breaks at last his darts—
You men, remember Christ with mind still sounding
'heave'.

Supreme, of virtues King, and fount of things,
He promises in strife, gives prize in victory —
You men, remember Christ with mind still sounding
'heave'.

V

God And The Devil

It's evil
to shun the King of righteousness
and make compact with demon.

VI

Winter

News I bring:
bells the stag,
winter snow,
summer past;

gáeth ard úar,
ísel grían,
gair a rith,
ruirthech rían;

rorúad rath,
ro-cleth cruth,
ro-gab gnáth
giugrann guth;

ro-gab úacht
etti én,
aigre ré:
é mo scél.

VII

Tair Cucum, a Maire Boíd
BLATHMAC MAC CON BRETTAN

Tair cucum, a Maire boíd,
do choíniuth frit do rochoím;
dirsan dul fri croich dot mac
ba mind már, ba masgérat.

Co tochmurr frit mo di láim
ar do macind irgabáil:
Ísu con-atoí do brú,
nícon fochmai th'ógai-siu.

       *   *   *

12

wind high and cold,
low the sun,
short its course,
seas run strong;

russet bracken,
shape awry,
wild goose raises
wonted cry;

cold lays hold
on wings of bird,
icy time:
this I heard.

VII

To Mary And Her Son
BLATHMAC SON OF CÚ BRETTAN

Come to me, loving Mary,
that I may keen with you your very dear one;
Alas! The going to the cross of your son,
that great jewel, that beautiful champion.

That with you I may beat my two hands
for your fair son's captivity.
Your womb has conceived Jesus —
it has not marred your virginity.

*   *   *

Cotn-abairt cen phecath fir,
do-forsat cen chneid ngalair;
rot-nert cen chumaid — cain rath! —
isind aimsir hi crochad.

Cair, in cúalaid mac am-ne
con-meseth a tréde-se?
Ní tuidchid for lesa ban
ocus nícon gignethar.

Prímgein Dé Athar fri nem
do mac, a Maire ingen;
ro-láithreth hi combairt glain
tri rath spirto sechtndelbaig.

Nícon fúair athair samlai,
a Maire, do macamrai;
ferr fáith, fisidiu cech druí,
rí ba hepscop, ba lánsuí.

Sainemlu cech dóen a chruth,
brestu cech sóer a balcbruth,
gaíthiu cech bruinniu fo nim,
fíriánu cech breithemain.

Maisiu, meldchu, mó macaib;
ó boí ina becbrataib
ru-fes a ndo-regad de,
gein tesairgne sochuide.

You have conceived him and no sin with man,
you brought him forth without ailing wound;
without grief he strengthened you (fair grace!)
at the time of his crucifixion.

I ask: Have you heard of a son like this,
one who could do these three things?
Such has not come upon the thighs of women
and such will not be born.

The first-begotten of God, the Father, in heaven
is your son, Mary, virgin;
he was begotten in a pure conception
through the power of the septiform Spirit.

No father has found, Mary,
the like of your renowned son;
better he than prophet, wiser than druid,
a king who was bishop and full sage.

His form was finer than that of other beings,
his stout vigour greater than any craftsman's,
wiser he than any breast under heaven,
juster than any judge.

More beautiful, more pleasant, bigger than other boys
since he was in his swaddling clothes;
it was known what would come of him,
a being for the saving of multitudes.

Sóer a ngein ro-génair úait,
rot-rath, a Maire, mórbúaid;
Críst mac Dé Athar do nim,
é ron-ucais i mBeithil.

*   *   *

Rom-bet mo théor aicdi lat,
a Maire mass muingelnat;
at-ethae, a grian na mban,
ót mac conid-midethar.

Mo buith for bith comba sen
la fíadait follnas rindnem,
ocus fáilte frium iar sin
isin mbithflaith mbithsuthain.

Cech óen díamba figel se
fo lige ocus éirge
ar imdídnad dianim tall
amail lúirech co cathbarr.

Cách nod-géba do cach deilb
i troscud aidchi Sathairnn
acht rob fo déraib cen meth,
a Maire, níb ifernach.

Fri tuidecht do maic co feirc
cona chroich fria ais imdeirc,
ara soírthar lat in tan
nach carae nod-coínfedar.

Noble the being born from you!
You were granted, Mary, a great gift:
Christ, son of the Father in heaven,
him have you borne in Bethlehem.

*   *   *

May I have from you my three petitions,
beautiful Mary, little white-necked one;
get them, sun amongst women,
from your son who has them in his power.

That I may be in the world till old
serving the Lord who rules starry heaven,
and that then there be a welcome for me
into the eternal, ever-enduring kingdom.

That everyone who uses this as a vigil prayer
at lying down and at rising,
that it may protect him from blemish in the other world
like a breastplate and helmet.

Everyone of any sort who shall recite it
fasting on Friday night,
provided only that it be with full-flowing tears,
Mary, may he not be for hell.

When your son comes in anger
with his cross on his reddened back,
that then you will save
any friend who shall have keened him.

Airiut, a Maire co llí,
rega-sa i n-aitiri:
cách gébas in coíniud nglan
ra-mbiä a thuarastal.

Dot-gaur co foclaib fíraib,
a Maire, a maisrígain,
con roirem cobrai ma tú
do airchisecht do chridi-siu.

Conro-choíner Críst as glé
frit-su tucht bas n-incride,
a lie lógmar laindrech,
a máthair in mórchoimdeth.

Ce chon-messinn co cach rían
doíni betho fo móenmíad
do-regtis lim ocus lat
conro-choíntis do rígmac.

Do lámchomairt cen moraich
mnáib macaib ferolaib
conro-choíntis for cach dind
ríg do-rósat cach n-óenrind.

Nacha cumgaim; ciche féin
do mac frit-su co daigléir
acht do-dichis-siu nach ré
do chélidiu cucum-sae.

For you, beautiful Mary,
I shall go as guarantor:
anyone who says the full keen,
he shall have his reward.

I call you with true words,
Mary, beautiful queen,
that we may have talk together
to pity your heart's darling.

So that I may keen the bright Christ
with you in the most heartfelt way,
shining precious jewel,
mother of the great Lord.

Were I rich and honoured
ruling the people of the world to every sea,
they would all come with you and me
to keen your royal son.

There would be beating of hands
by women, children and men,
that they might keen on every hill-top
the king who made every star.

I cannot do this. With heartfelt feeling
I will bewail your son with you
if only you come at some time
on a visit to me.

Do airchisecht chridi cen on
con roirem ar ndiabor,
a chond na creitme glaine,
tair cucum, a boídMaire.

VIII

Caoineadh Na Maighdine

'Is mithid dom', arsan Mhaighdean, 'dul ag fiosrú mo
    ghrádh geal'
    (Och! Ochón agus ochón ó).
Do bhí a ceann scaoilte is a cosa gan náda
    (Och! Ochón agus ochón ó),
isí ag bailiú a chuid fola ós cionn an fhásaigh
    (Och! Ochón agus ochón ó).

Do léim sí isteach is amach thar ghárda
    (Och! Ochón agus ochón ó).
'Dia dhuit, a mhic, nó an aithnid duit do mháthair'
    (Och! Ochón agus ochón ó).
'Bíodh agat an fhoidhne agus geobhaidh tú na grásta'
    (Och! Ochón agus ochón ó).
'A leinbh, is mór é t'ualach is leig cuid de ar do mháthair'
    (Och! Ochón agus ochón ó).
'Iomchruigheadh gach n-aon a chrosa féin agus
    iomchróchad-sa thar ceann sliocht Adhaimh é'
    (Och! Ochón agus ochón ó).

Come to me, loving Mary,
you, head of unsullied faith,
that we may have talk together
with the compassion of unblemished heart.

VIII

The Virgin's Lament

Said the Virgin: 'Let me go to be with my bright darling'
        (Och! Ochone and Ochone O).
Her hair was flying and her feet were bare
        (Och! Ochone and Ochone O),
and she gathering his blood in the desert place
        (Och! Ochone and Ochone O).

She sprang in and out through the guarding soldiers
        (Och! Ochone and Ochone O).
'Bless you my son, do you know your own mother?'
        (Och! Ochone and Ochone O).
'Have patience, mother and you will get all graces'
        (Och! Ochone and Ochone O).
'O child, it's a heavy burden, let your mother part bear it'
        (Och! Ochone and Ochone O).
'To each his own cross, for me that of Adam's children'
        (Och! Ochone and Ochone O).

IX
Dom-farcai Fidbaidæ Fál

Dom-farcai fidbaidæ fál,
    fom-chain loíd luin — lúad nad cél;
húas mo lebrán, ind línech,
    fom-chain trírech inna n-én.

Fomm-chain coí menn — medair mass —
    hi mbrot glass de dindgnaib doss.
Débrad! nom-choimmdiu coíma,
    caín-scríbaimm fo foída ross.

X
Is Acher In Gáith In-Nocht

Is acher in gáith in-nocht,
fu-fúasna fairggæ findfolt:
ní ágor réimm mora minn
dond láechraid lainn úa Lothlind.

XI
Fuitt Co Bráth

Fuitt co bráth!
    Is mó in doinenn ar cách;
is ob cach etriche án,
    ocus is loch lán cach áth.

IX

Writing Out Of Doors

A wall of forest looms above
    and sweetly the blackbird sings;
all the birds make melody
    over me and my books and things.

There sings to me the cuckoo
    from bush-citadels in grey hood.
God's doom! May the Lord protect me
    writing well, under the great wood.

X

The Vikings

Bitter and wild is the wind to-night
tossing the tresses of the sea to white.
On such a night as this I feel at ease:
fierce Northmen only course the quiet seas.

XI

Forever Cold

Forever cold!
Weather grim and grimmer still,
glittering brook a river
and ford a brimming lake.

Is méit muir mór cech loch lonn,
    is drong cech cuire gúr gann,
méit taul scéith banna dond linn,
    méit moltchrocann finn cech slamm.

Méit cuithe cach lathrach léig,
    coirthe cach réid, caill cach móin,
inna helta, nís tá dín,
    snechtae finn fír do-roich tóin.

Ro-íad réod rótu gribb
    iar ngléo glicc im choirthi Cuilt,
con-gab domenn dar cach leth
    coná apair nech acht 'Fuitt'.

XII
Batar Inmuini Trí Toíb

Batar inmuini trí toíb
    frisná fresciu aitherrech,
tóebán Temro, toíb Taillten,
    toíb Áedo maicc Ainmirech.

XIII
Cen Áinius

Cen áinius
in gním í do-rigénus,
an ro-carus ro-cráidius.

The lake a great sea
(each meagre band a company)
rain-drop like shield-boss
and snow-flake like wether-skin.

The dirty puddle is a great pit,
level land is risen, the moor a wood,
no shelter for the flocks of birds
and white snow reaches up to haunch.

Sudden frost has closed the roads
encircling with cunning the standing-stone at Colt;
grim weather lies entrenched on every side
and no one utters anything but: 'Cold'.

XII
Áed Mac Ainmirech

Beloved were three sides
I cannot hope to see again,
side of Tara, side of Tailltiu,
side of Áed mac Ainmirech.

XIII
Líadan's Lament

No pleasure
that deed I did, tormenting him,
tormenting what I treasure.

Ba mire
nád dernad a airer-som
mainbed ómun ríg nime.

Níbu amlos
dó-som in dál dúthracair,
ascnam sech phéin i Pardos.

Bec mbríge
ro-chráidi frimm Cuirithir,
fris-sium ba mór mo míne.

Mé Líadan —
ro-carus-sa Cuirithir,
is fírinne ad-fíadar.

Gair bá-sa
i comaitecht Chuirithir,
fris-sium ba maith mo gnássa.

Céol caille
fom-chanad la Cuirithir
la fogur fairrge flainne.

Do-ménainn
ní cráidfed frimm Cuirithir
do dálaib cacha dénainn.

Ní chela:
ba hé-sium mo chrideserc
cía no carainn cách cena.

Joyfully
but that God had come between us then
had I granted what he begged of me.

Not unwise
is the way that he is taking now,
enduring pain and gaining Paradise.

Great folly
where once I showed such gentleness
to set Cuirithir against me!

Líadan I;
they say that I loved Cuirithir,
nor would I, if I could, deny.

The while I bless
that I was in his company
and was treating him with tenderness.

A woodland breeze
was my melody with Cuirithir
sounding harmony of reddening seas.

It seemed thus:
the last thing I would ever do
was a deed to come between us.

Cry clearly:
if any lovers this heart cherishes,
he its darling, loved most dearly.

27

Deilm ndega
ro-tethainn mo chride-se,
ro-fess nícon bía cena.

XIV

Cride Hé

Cride hé,
    daire cnó,
ócán é,
    pócán dó.

XV

Aithbe Dam Cen Bés Moro

Aithbe dam cen bés moro —
    sentu fom-dera croan;
toirse oca cía dono? —
    sona do-táet a loan.

Is mé caillech Bérri Buí,
no-meilinn léini mbithnuí;
indíu táthum do séimi
ná melainn cid aithléini.

A cry of pain
and the heart within was rent in two,
without him never beats again.

XIV

Tender Lad

Tender lad,
    a darling this,
grove of nuts,
    worth a kiss.

XV

Ebbing

The ebbing that has come on me
is not the ebbing of the sea.
What knows the sea of grief or pain? —
Happy tide will flood again.

I am the hag of Buí and Beare —
the richest cloth I used to wear.
Now with meanness and with thrift
I even lack a change of shift.

It moíni
cartar lib, nídat doíni;
sinni, indbaid marsaimme
batar doíni carsaimme.

Batar inmaini doíni
    ata maige mad-ríadam;
ba maith no-mcilmis leo,
    ba becc no-mmoítis íaram.

Indíu trá cáin timgarat
    ocus ní mór nond-oídet;
cíasu becc do-n-indnagat
    is mór a mét no-mmoídet.

Carpait lúaith
ocus eich no beirtis búaid,
ro boí, denus, tuile díb;
bennacht ar ríg do-da-úaid.

Tocair mo chorp co n-aichri
    dochum adba dían aithgni;
tan bas mithig la mac nDé
    do-té do brith a aithni.

Ó do-éctar mo láma
    ot é cnámacha cáela,
nítat fíu turcbáil, taccu,
    súas tar na maccu cáema.

It is wealth
and not men that you love.
In the time that we lived
it was men that we loved.

Those whom we loved, the plains
we ride today bear their names;
gaily they feasted with laughter
nor boasted thereafter.

To-day they gather in the tax
but, come to handing out, are lax;
the very little they bestow
be sure that everyone will know.

Chariots there were, and we
had horses bred for victory.
Such things came in a great wave;
pray for the dead kings who gave.

Bitterly does my body race
seeking its destined place;
now let God's Son come and take
that which he gave of his grace.

These arms, these scrawny things you see,
    scarce merit now their little joy
when lifted up in blessing
    over sweet student boy.

31

Ot é cnámacha cáela
    ó do-éctar mo láma,
ba inmainiu tan gnítis
    bítis im ríga rána.

It fáilti na ingena
    ó thic dóib co Beltaine;
is deithbiriu dam-sa brón,
    sech am tróg, am sentainne.

Ní feraim cobrai milis,
    ní marbtar muilt dom banais;
is becc, is líath mo thrilis,
    ní líach droch-caille tarais.

Ní olc lium
ce beith caille finn form chiunn;
boí móirmeither cech datha
form chiunn oc ól dag-latha.

Ním-gaib format fri nach sen
inge nammá fri Feimen:
meisse, rom-melt forbaid sin,
buide beus barr Feimin.

Lia na Ríg hi Femun,
Caithir Rónáin hi mBregun,
cían ó ro-s-siachtat sína,
a lleicne nít sen-chrína.

These arms you see,
        these bony scrawny things,
had once more loving craft
        embracing kings.

When Maytime comes
        the girls out there are glad,
and I, old hag, old bones,
        alone am sad.

No wedding wether killed for me,
an end to all coquetry;
a pitiful veil I wear
on thin and faded hair.

Well do I wear
plain veil on faded hair;
many colours I wore
and we feasting before.

Were it not for Feven's plain
        I'd envy nothing old;
I have a shroud of aged skin,
        Feven's crop is gold.

Ronan's city there in Bregon
        and in Feven the royal standing stone,
why are their cheeks not weathered,
        only mine alone?

33

Is labar tonn moro máir,
ros-gab in gaim cumgabáil;
fer maith, mac mogo in-díu
ní freiscim do chéilidiu.

Is éol dam a ndo-gniat,
    rait ocus do-raat;
curchasa Átha Alma,
    is úar ind adba hi faat.

Is mó láu
nád muir n-oíted imma-ráu;
testa már mblíadnae dom chruth,
dáig fo-rroimled mo chétluth.

Is mó dé
dam-sa in-díu, cibé de;
gaibthium étach cid fri gréin,
do-fil áes dam, at-gén féin.

Sam oíted i rrabamar
do-miult cona fagamur;
gaim aís báides cech nduine,
domm-ánaic a fochmuine.

Ro-miult m'oítid ar thuus
is buide lem ron-gleus;
cid becc mo léim dar duae
níbu nuae in bratt beus.

Winter comes and the sea will rise
    crying out with welcoming wave;
but no welcome for me from nobleman's son
    or from son of a slave.

What they do now, I know, I know:
    to and fro they row and race;
but they who once sailed Alma's ford
    rest in a cold place.

It's more than a day
    since I sailed youth's sea,
beauty's years not devoured
    and sap flowing free.

It's more than a day, God's truth,
that I'm lacking in youth;
I wrap myself up in the sun —
I know Old Age, I see him come.

There was a summer of youth
    nor was autumn the worst of the year,
but winter is doom
    and its first days are here.

God be thanked, I had joy of my youth.
    I swear that it's true,
if I hadn't leapt the wall
    this old cloak still were not new.

Is álainn in bratt úaine
    ro-scar mo Rí tar dromman;
is sáer in Fer no-d-lúaidi:
    do-rat loí fair íar lommad.

Aminecán morúar dam
    — cech n-érchaín is erchraide —
íar feis fri caindlib sorchaib
    bith i ndorchuib derthaige!

Rom-boí denus la ríga
oc ól meda ocus fína;
    indíu ibim medcuisce
eter sentainni crína.

Rop ed mo choirm: cóid in midc,
    ropo toil Dé cecham-theirp
oc do guidi-siu, a Dé bí,
    do-rat a chró clí fri feirg.

Ad-cíu form brott brodrad n-aís,
ro-gab mo chíall mo thogaís;
líath a finn ásas trim thoinn,
is samlaid crotball senchruinn.

Rucad úaim-se mo súil des
día reic ar thír mbithdíles;
ocus rucad int súil chlé
do formach a foirdílse.

36

The Lord on the world's broad back
    threw a lovely cloak of green;
first fleecy, then it's bare,
    and again the fleece is seen.

All beauty is doomed.
    God! Can it be right
to kneel in a dark prayer-house
    after feasting by candlelight?

I sat with kings drinking wine and mead
    for many a day,
and now, a crew of shrivelled hags,
    we toast in whey.

Be this my feast, these cups of whey;
    and let me always count as good
the vexing things that come of Christ
    who stayed God's ire with flesh and blood.

The mind is not so clear,
    there's mottling of age on my cloak,
grey hairs sprouting through skin,
    I am like a stricken oak.

For deposit on heaven
    of right eye bereft,
I concluded the purchase
    with loss of the left.

Tonn tuili
  ocus ind í aithbi áin,
a ndo-beir tonn tuili dait
  beirid tonn aithbi as do láim.

Tonn tuili
  ocus ind aile aithbi,
dom-áncatar-sa uili
  conda éola a n-aithgni.

Tonn tuili
ní cos tar socht mo chuili;
  cid mór mo dám fo deimi
fo-cress lám forru uili.

Mad ro-feissed mac Maire
  co mbeith fo chlí mo chuile:
cení dernus gart cenae
  ní érburt 'nac' fri duine.

Tróg n-uile! —
  doíriu dúilib don duiniu
nád ndecha asind aithbiu-se
  feib do-ndecha asin tuiliu.

Mo thuile,
  is maith con-roíter m'aithne;
ra-sóer Ísu mac Maire
  conda toirsech co aithbe.

Great wave of flood
    and wave of ebb and lack!
What flooding tide brings in
        the ebbing tide takes back.

Great wave of flood
    and wave of ebbing sea,
the two of them I know
        for both have washed on me.

Great wave of flood
    brings no step to silent cellar floor;
a hand fell on all the company
        that feasted there before.

The Son of Mary knew right well
    he'd walk that floor one day;
grasping I was, but never sent
        man hungry on his way.

Pity Man! —
    If only like the elements he could
come out of ebbing in the very way
        that he comes out of flood.

Christ left with me on loan
    flood tide of youth, and now it seems
there's ebb and misery, for Mary's Son
        too soon redeems.

Céin mair ailén mora máir,
dosn-ic tuile íarna tráig;
os mé, ní frescu dom-í
tuile tar éisi n-aithbi.

XVI

Fégaid Úaib

Fégaid úaib
sair fo thúaid
in muir múaid
    mílach;
adba rón
rebach, rán,
ro-gab lán
    línad.

XVII

Ná Luig, Ná Luig

Ná luig, ná luig
    fót fora taí:
gairit bía fair,
    fota bía faí.

Blessed the island in the great sea
    with happy ebb and happy flood.
For me, for me alone, no hope:
    the ebbing is for good.

XVI

The Sea

Look you out
northeastwards
over mighty ocean,
    teeming with sea-life;
home of seals,
sporting, splendid,
its tide has reached
    fullness.

XVII

The World

Take no oath, take no oath
    by the sod you stand upon:
you walk it short while
    but your burial is long.

Ná len, ná len
    in domun cé,
ná car, ná car,
    sel bec a ré.

Ná sir, ná sir
    in saegul seng,
ná gab, ná gab,
    ná tuit 'na chenn.

Baí sunn indé,
    ba gel a gné,
ní fil indiu
    acht 'na chrú fó chré.

Atá 'na rith
    mar théit in muir,
teich úaid i céin,
    ná héir, ná luig.

XVIII

M'áenurán Dam Isa Slíab

M'áenurán dam isa slíab,
    a rí grían rob soraid sét;
ním nessa éc ina meing
    indás no beinn tríchait chét.

Pay no heed, pay no heed
    to the world and its way,
give no love, give no love
    to what lasts but a day.

Have no care, have no care
    for the meaningless earth,
lay not hold, lay not hold
    on its gaiety and mirth.

A man fair of face
    was here yesterday;
now he is nothing
    but blood beneath clay.

The world is running out
    like the ebbing sea:
fly far from it
    and seek safety.

XVIII

Fate

I walk the lonely mountain road —
my King of Suns — and darkest glen,
no nearer death, though I be alone,
than fared I with three thousand men.

Cía no beinn-sea tríchait chét
        dind ócbaid tét, tenna a cnis,
dia tí caingen in báis brais
        ní fil daingen gabas fris.

Ní fil inill i nach dú
do mac duini acht rob trú:
ní cúala nech díambad toich
        belach fors ngondais étroich.

Cía dúthraigid nech mo brath,
cid santach imm scribulrath,
nó corob dén fíadat finn,
cía im-ráidi, ní cumaing.

Ní cumaing duinén in-díu
mo sáegul do thimdibiu,
acht in rí ro-delb in sam,
coimmdiu nime ocus talman.

Ním derban do thecht for fecht
cía sréidid nech i n-airecht;
fót for ro-delbad mo lecht,
isam écen a thairecht,

Ním derban d'imthecht m'áenur,
        sáegul rom delba, ním roisc;
ní tíag don biuth corba trú,
        ní tuit in cnú corba foisc.

Though fared I forth three thousand strong,
all lusty lads with bodies tough,
and mighty death came stalking me,
would they ward him off, were they enough?

If one be fey there's no safe place
and seeking sanctuary is vain,
while seems to me scarce natural
a path whereon the undoomed are slain.

A man may think to take my life,
appropriate my purse and pence,
but till the fair Lord gives assent
he'll plot and plan, and I'll not hence.

Where today stands any man
with power to snatch my life away?
None but the Maker of earth and sky,
the Shaper of the Summer-day.

Signs do not stop me setting out
— Did someone sneeze? — for my last breath
will be when foot compulsively
treads the awaiting sod of death.

I fear no more to walk alone;
let world which shaped me, gave me birth,
take not untimely back but wait
for nut-ripe falling to the earth.

In láech renas a chneas mbán
    isind áth fri galus ngúr,
ní nessa dó éc, cid báeth,
    indás don gáeth bís ar cúl.

Cía dú do fiur chonaire
    cuingid comairge for sét?
Isin chomairgi do-thét
    cate a chomairge ar éc?

Aminecán! Cía dono
do neuch imgabáil gono;
tairic a laithe báeguil
do chách i ciunn a śáeguil

For fáesam Dé uasail áin,
    athair noí ngrád spirut nóeb,
ním reilce i n-úathaib báis báin
    nó i ngráin cía dom-ecma im óen.

XIX

Flamina Nos Boreae
SEDULIUS SCOTTUS

Flamina nos Boreae miro canentia vultu
    Perterrent subitis motibus atque minis:
Tellus ipsa tremit nimio perculsa pavore,
    Murmurat et pelagus duraque saxa gemunt,

The lad who risks his shining skin
in that ford yonder opposing might,
must he, then, be nearer death
than the skulker from the fight?

And why this seeking company?
Is it, perhaps, that you
are set on scaring death away
in awe of a great retinue?

Indeed, indeed, avoiding death
takes too much time and too much care,
and then, at the end of all,
he catches each one unaware.

May nine ranks of angels and my God
be ever watchful over me,
from terror, from caverns of white death
protecting, bearing company.

XIX

The Arrival at Liège
SEDULIUS SCOTTUS

Dread-visaged Boreas blows rimy blasts and we
shrink back in terror from sudden darts and threats;
trembling the land, white-stricken with great fear,
and sea cries out and the hard rocks moan;

Aereos tractus Aquilo nunc vastat iniquus
    Vocibus horrisonis murmuribusque tonans,
Lactea nubifero densantur vellera caelo,
    Velatur nivea marcida terra stola,
Labuntur subito silvoso vertice crines
    Nec stat harundineo robur et omne modo,
Titan, clarifico qui resplendebat amictu,
    Abscondit radios nunc faciemque suam.
Nos tumidus Boreas vastat — miserabile visu —
    Doctos grammaticos presbiterosque pios:
Namque volansAquilo non ulli parcit honori
    Crudeli rostro nos laniando suo. —

Fessis ergo favens, Hartgari floride praesul,
    Sophos Scottigenas suscipe corde pio:
Scandere sic valeas caelestia templa beatus,
    Aetheream Solimam perpetuamque Sion.

Praesulis eximii clementia mensque serena
    Flamina devicit rite superba domans.
Suscepit blandus fessosque loquacibus austris
    Eripuit ternos dapsilitate sophas;
Et nos vestivit, triplici ditavit honore
    Et fecit proprias pastor amoenus oves.

now he menaces the spaces of the air
with dread-arousing cries and thundering roar;
sky's milky fleece is covered with glowering cloud
and earth stands pallid in a snow-white gown;
and suddenly the woodland sheds its hair,
stout oak starts shaking like a reed;
the sun, that once had shone resplendently,
withholds his rays, now wholly hides his face;
ah woe! tumultuous Boreas has us all undone,
we learned teachers, yes, and pious priests,
for eagle Northwind has no regard of state
and mangles even us with cruel beak.

Then, Hartgar, powerful prelate, raise the weak,
cherish the learned Irish with gentle heart,
so, blessed, in heaven's high temples may you walk,
celestial Jerusalem and enduring Zion.

Great prelate! His mercy and his quiet mind
conquered the blasts and tamed old Boreas' pride;
kindly he led the weary in, and bountiful
snatched three scholars from the howling winds,
clothing us and honouring all three
so we became that gentle shepherd's sheep.

XX

Vestri Tecta Nitent Luce Serena

Vestri tecta nitent luce serena;
Florent arte nova culmina picta;
Rident atque tolo multicolora
Et formosa micant scemata plura.
Non sic, Hesperidum hortule, flores,
Marcescis subitis qui cito dampnis:
Nam vestrae violae seu rosa pulchra
Inhaesere tolis perpete sede;
Sic ostrum rubeum, sic iacincthus
Non horrent tumidi flamina Nothi.

Nostri tecta nigrant perpete nocte;
Intus nulla nitet gratia lucis;
Pictae vestis abest pulchra venustas;
Clavis nulla regit ac sera nulla;
Absis nonque micat compta tabellis —
Sed fuligo tolo haeret in alto;
Si, Neptune, pluas imbribus atris,
Crebras rore gravi domata nostra;
Eurus si reboet murmure saevo,
Haec quassata tremit aula vetusta.

Caci talis erat mansio tetra;
Talis caecus erat iam Laborintus,
Instar qui fuerat noctis opacae.
Sic et nostra domus — heu nefas ingens —
Horret palliolo fuscida nigro:

XX

Hartgar's Palace
SEDULIUS SCOTTUS

Your halls are gleaming with a light serene
and latest style in art adorns the scene
with beauteous forms to populate your home
and many merry colours in your dome;
a garden of Hesperides each room
with flowers dancing in perpetual bloom,
the rose, the violets that never die
but cling to wall and cupola on high:
the withering southern blast may blow and blow
and purple, red or jacinth never know.

It's different where we live: perpetual night
within the house and ne'er a gleam of light;
no florid beauty decorates the walls,
no key nor bar protects us in our halls;
arches lack paint and scenic gaiety but
the ceiling has a pattern of soot.
Ah! Neptune, when you send us those dark showers
a heavy dew invades this house of ours;
be quiet, East Wind, nor raise your voice at all
or else the walls near tumble on us all.

A loathsome cave had Cacus, Vulcan's boy,
a labyrinth devoid of light and joy,
night's very image, full of dark and fear;
to put in brief — Ah, woe! — 'twas just like here.

Nam lucente die noctis imago
Crassescit vetulis aedibus istis.
Non haec apta domus, crede, sophistis,
Qui splendentis amant munera lucis —
Sed haec apta domus nicticoraci
Talparumque gregi mansio digna.
O Lantberte, nigros collige caecos
Omnes, oro, tuos transfer in istam:
Caecorum valeat semper in aevum
Haec obscura domus rite vocari.

Sed nunc, celse pater splendide pastor,
His succurre malis, o decus almum;
Dic verboque pio, quo decoretur
Haec umbrosa domus priva dierum:
Sit pulchrum laquear stigmate pictum;
Sit clavisque recens ac sera firma;
Mox glaucae, vitreae sintque fenestrae,
Quo Phebus radios dirigat almus
Perlustretque sophos crine decoro,
Praesul clare, tuos lucis amantes.

XXI

Nunc Viridant Segetes

Nunc viridant segetes, nunc florent germine campi,
Nunc turgent vites, est nunc pulcherrimus annus,
Nunc pictae volucres permulcent aethera cantu,
Nunc mare, nunc tellus, nunc caeli sidera rident.

Our dwelling shudders in a cloak of black.
When daylight comes she promptly sends it back,
grows ever blacker and assumes a guise
not fit, I say, for scholars or the wise,
such as love splendour and the gifts of light,
but more for moles and owls and things of night.
Oh, Hartgar! All such that cannot see
gather together and bring them here to me —
for this dark house a fitting use we'll find.
We'll christen it: 'Asylum for the Blind.'

Or else, great father, pastor with power and might,
come to our aid and set these matters right,
speaking the gracious word that workmen may
start on the job, let in the light of day;
first figures on ceiling paint, and we
have need of bar and bolt, have need of key;
then windows gleaming bright with sparkling glass
in such a way that rays of light may pass
shining for scholars, and warming hearts that do
but love, my lord, the light and sun and you.

XXI

Request For Meat And Drink
SEDULIUS SCOTTUS

The crops are green and fields are all in flower,
budding the vine — the year now has its hour;
gay-painted songbirds fill the air with glee,
there's smile on land and sky and laughs the sea.

Ast nos tristificis perturbat potio sucis,
Cum medus atque Ceres, cum Bachi munera desint;
Heu — quam multiplicis defit substantia carnis,
Quam mitis tellus generat, quam roscidus aether.

Scriptor sum (fateor), sum Musicus alter et Orpheus,
Sum bos triturans, prospera quaeque volo,
Sum vester miles sophiae praeditus armis:
Pro nobis nostrum, Musa, rogato patrem.

XXII

De Strage Normannorum

Gaudeant caeli, mare, cuncta terra,
Gaudeat Christi populusque vernans;
Facta miretur domini tonantis
    Fortia patris.

Laudibus dignus bonitatis auctor,
Magnus in magnis opifex beatus,
Cuncta dispensat dominante nutu
    Sceptriger orbis.

Spes, salus mundi, pius ipse rector
Conterens pravos humiles coronat,
Sublevat valles reprimitque montes
    Celsa potestas.

Of mirth-provoking sap I too have need,
some beer, or Bacchus' gift, or perhaps some mead;
and then there's meat, produce of earth and sky,
and I have none, but ask the reason why.

Now, Muse, I write and sing, am Orpheus reborn,
but too have needs, the ox that treads the corn;
your champion I, with wisdom's arms I fight:
Off to the bishop, and tell him of my plight.

XXII

Defeat Of The Northmen
SEDULIUS SCOTTUS

Rejoice you heavens, sea and all the land;
you people too who flower in Christ,
see the great deeds of the Lord, the Father,
    thundering Godhead.

Most worthy of praises, sole author of good,
great in great deeds, blessed creator,
holding firmament's sceptre and with nod of the brow
    all things disposing.

World's holy ruler, its hope and salvation,
levelling mountain, raising the valley,
crushing the wicked, crowning the humble,
    omnipotent power.

Qui facit rectis radiare verum
Lumen in cordis speculoque mentis,
Quos tegit semper pietate pollens
    Conditor almus.

Pauperes, dites, laici, potentes,
O coronate clericalis ordo,
Omnis aetatis decus atque sexus,
    Plaudite cuncti.

Brachium patris validum potentis
Ecce protrivit subita rebellem
Strage Normannum pietatis hostem:
    Gloria patri.

Proelium campo struitur patenti,
Splendor armorum radiat per auras,
Voce bellantum varia tremescit
    Machina caeli.

Tela sparserunt geminae phalanges,
Danus infelix sua dampna quaerit,
Ferreos imbres serit atque fixit
    Agmen inorme.

Quem sitiverunt varios per annos
Sanguinem sumunt rabidi tyranni:
Dulce fit cunctis satiare pectus
    Caede virorum.

Christ the true Light He causes to shine
on faithful hearts, on mirror of the mind,
cherishing them with constancy,
    sustaining creator.

You rich and poor, you high and humble,
clerics too, His tonsured order,
young and old, mankind and women,
    praise Him you all.

The stout strong arm of a powerful father
with sudden fury has now prostrated
foes of the faithful, the rebel Northman;
    glory to the Father.

The fight is joined on open plain
and weapons glitter in the limpid air
and warrior cry might seem to shake
    the scaffolding of sky.

Opposing lines unleash their spearshafts,
unhappy Northman counts his losses,
a mighty army aims and places
    its showers of iron.

Those who have thirsted down through the years
are quaffing the blood of a savage oppressor
and finding sweet savour in nourishing heart
    on the slaughter of men.

Quique foderunt foveas, ruere;
Quae fuit turris nimium superba,
Ecce curvatur nihilata Christo
    Gens inimica.

Sternitur grandis populusque fortis,
Tota contrita est maledicta massa,
Sorbet os mortis sobolem malignam:
    Laus tibi, Christe.

Hinc ferunt stragem populi fuisse:
Praeter ignotos hominesque vilis
Horrido campo nimio cruore
    Tres myriades.

Justus est iudex dominator orbis,
Christianorum decus omne Christus,
Gloriae princeps, domitor malorum
    Regmine summo.

Fortis est turris, clipeus salutis
Conterens bello validos gigantes,
Cuius excelsum super omne nomen
    Est benedictum.

Ultor existit populi fidelis,
Qui maris quondam tumidis procellis
Pressit Aegyptum, celeres rotasque
    Obruit imo.

Those who set snares stand there ensnared,
topples a tower reaching to the sky;
a hostile horde, swelling with pride,
    Christ has undone them.

There is there laid low a stout strong people,
a cursed mass has now been crumbled,
an evil issue death's maw has swallowed;
    be praised, O Christ.

Now can be reckoned a mighty slaughter:
count not unknown, count not the menials,
on that dread field lay bloody there
    three times ten thousand.

The judge is just, lord of the world,
Christ the true glory of Christian people,
magnificent ruler, vanquishing evil
    in high jurisdiction.

Great tower is He, and shield of salvation
undoing in battle the strength of the giants,
Whose name is high above all names
    and ever blessed.

A faithful people has that great avenger
who unleashed the sea in swelling torrents
on proud Egyptian, overwhelming all,
    chariots, horsemen.

Ostriger Jesus super omne regnat,
Quicquid excelsus genitor creavit,
Stirpe Davidis benedicta proles,
    Gloria nostra.

Cui rependatur tymiama voti,
Quem celebremus pietatis actu,
Cui melos promat super astra regi
    Fistula laudis.

Gloriae plausus, modulans osanna
Personet patrem genitumque Christum,
Spiritum sanctum: polus unda tellus,
    Glorificate.

XXIII

Justus Quid Meruit

Justus quid meruit, simplex, sine fraude maligna?
    Munera nec Bachi, non siceramque bibit,
Non hunc ebrietas deflexit tramite recti,
    Non epulae regum nec procerumque dapes:
Illi pastus erat sollemnicus herba per agros
    Ac dulcem potum limphida Mosa dabat:
Non ostri vestes rubei cupiebat avarus,
    Sed contentus erat pellicia tunica;
Nonque superbus equo lustrabat amoena virecta
    Sed propriis pedibus rite migrabat iter;
Non mendosus erat nec inania verba loquutus:
    Báá seu béé mystica verba dabat.

Christ wearing purple now reigns over
what high Begetter first created,
blessed scion of the House of David
    and our glory.

He to Whom we offer incense,
Whom we name in act of prayer,
King of stars Whom we intone
    on pipe of praise.

Now cry you glory and cry Hosanna,
now sing of Father, Christ begotten,
and Holy Spirit; sky, earth and water
    praise Him you all.

XXIII

On The Slaying of a Ram
SEDULIUS SCOTTUS

Wherein his guilt — so simple, straight and true?
Bacchus he shunned, sherbet avoided too;
not him did liquor from narrow path entice,
not meal with king, or lesser lord, his vice;
his solemn feast was grazing on the grass,
his sweetest drink from brink of limpid Maas,
nor did he plead that he be vested in
purple or red — felt happy with a skin;
and never did he ride astride a horse
but steady on his legs he plied a course,
lied not, nor idle word did ever say,
but utterance of depth — just 'baa' and 'beh'.

61

Tu, bone multo, vale, nivei gregis inclite ductor,
Heu quia nec vivum te meus hortus habet.
Forsan, amice, tibi fieret calidumque lavacrum —
Non alia causa, iure sed hospitii;
Ipse ministrassem devoto pectore limphas
Cornigero capita, calcibus atque tuis.
Te (fateor) cupii; viduam matremque cupisco,
Fratres atque tuos semper amabo. Vale.

XXIV
Aut Lego Vel Scribo

Aut lego vel scribo, doceo scrutorve sophiam:
Obsecro celsithronum nocte dieque meum.
Vescor, poto libens, rithmizans invoco Musas,
Dormisco stertens: oro deum vigilans.
Conscia mens scelerum deflet peccamina vitae:
Parcite vos misero, Christe Maria, viro.

XXV
In India

Ro- fess a maith as cech aird,
a magnéit, a hadamaint,
is a margréit a hur i n-or,
a hór is a carrmocol.

62

Adieu good chief of gleaming herd — alas!
  I see you not a-feeding on my grass.
  Ah! Were you there a hot bath I had planned
  (only to please the guest you understand!)
  and self would minister with devoted breast
  to head and horn and hoof and all the rest.
  You have I loved, and love your widow too,
  mother I love, and brothers all — Adieu.

XXIV

Confession
SEDULIUS SCOTTUS

I read and write and teach, philosophy peruse.
I eat and freely drink, with rhymes invoke the muse,
I call on heaven's throne both night and day,
snoring I sleep, or stay awake and pray.
And sin and fault inform each act I plan:
Ah! Christ and Mary, pity this miserable man.

XXV

India
AIRBERTACH MAC COISSE

  Its goods are known far and wide,
  its lodestone, its adamant,
  from land to land its pearls,
  its gold and its carbuncle.

63

A hóenbennach for cóe gnáith,
a ggáeth féthamail fírbláith,
a heliphaint co mbríg bil,
a búain fo dí in cach bliadain.

XXVI

Ísucán

Ísucán
    alar lemm im dísiurtán;
cía beth cléirech co lín sét
    is bréc uile acht Ísucán.

Altram alar lemm im thig
    ní altram nach dóerathaig;
Ísu co feraib nime
    frim chride cech n-óenadaig.

Ísucán óc mo bithmaith,
    ernaid ocus ní maithmech;
in rí con-ic na uili
    cen a guidi bid aithrech.

Ísu úasal ainglide,
    noco cléirech dergnaide;
alar lemm im dísiurtán
    Ísu mac na Ebraide.

Its unicorn on wonted path,
smooth and truly gentle breeze,
elephants with vicious power,
harvest twice in every year.

XXVI

St. Ite's Song

Ísucán,
I nurse him in my lonely place;
though a priest have stores of wealth,
all is vain save Ísucán.

The nursling fostered in my house
is no son of base-born churl;
Jesus comes with heavenly host
to my breast each even-tide.

Young Ísucán, my eternal good,
bestows, is not witholding;
woe to him who does not pray
the king with power in everything.

Jesus, noble, angel-like,
not a common priest is he;
I nurse, here in my lonely place,
Jesus, son of Jewish maiden.

Maic na ruirech, maic na ríg,
im thír cía do-ísatán,
ní úaidib saílim sochur,
is tochu lemm Ísucán.

Canaid cóir, a ingena,
d'fiur dliges bar císucán;
atá 'na phurt túasucán
cía beith im ucht Ísucán.

XXVII

Atá Uarboth Dam I Caill

Atá úarboth dam i caill,
nís-fitir acht mo Fhíada:
uinnius di-síu, coll an-all,
bile rátha nosn-íada.

Dí ersainn fraích fri fulong
ocus fordorus féithe;
feraid in chaill imma cress
a mess for mucca méithe.

Mét mo boithe: beccnat becc,
baile sétae sognath;
canaid sian mbinn día beinn
ben a lleinn co londath.

*   *   *

Sons of kings, both great and small,
may come this way to visit me;
but my profit is not in them,
I rather choose Ísucán.

Chant a choir-song, virgins
for him to whom your rent is due;
in his dwelling high above
and at my breast is Ísucán.

XXVII

The Hermit

I have a bothy in the wood —
none knows it but the Lord, my God;
one wall an ash, the other hazel,
and a great fern makes the door.

The doorsteps are of heather,
the lintel of honeysuckle;
and wild forest all around
drops mast for well-fed swine.

This size my hut: the smallest thing,
homestead amid well-trod paths;
a woman — blackbird clothed and coloured —
is singing sweetly from its gable.

*　　　*　　　*

Monga lebra ibair éoglais,
    nósta cél!
Caín in magan márglas darach
    darsin sén.

Aball ubull (már a ratha)
    mbruidnech mbras;
barr dess dornach, collán cnobecc
    cróebach nglas.

Glére thibrat, essa uisci,
    úais do dig;
bruinnit ilair, cáera ibair,
    fidait fir.

Foilgit impe mucca cenntai,
    cadlaid, uirc,
mucca alltai, oiss aird, eillti,
    bruicnech, bruic.

Buidnech, sídech, slúag tromm tírech,
    dál dom thig;
ina erchaill tecat cremthainn,
    álainn sin.

           *   *   *

Líne ugae, mil, mess, melle,
    Dia dod-roíd;
ubla milsi, mónainn derca,
    dercna froích.

           *   *   *

Smooth the tresses of yew-green yew-trees,
        glorious portent;
place delicious with great green oakwoods
        increasing blessing.

Tree of apples huge and magic,
        great its graces;
crop in fistfulls from clustered hazel,
        green and branching.

Sparkling wells and water-torrents,
        best for drinking;
green privet there and bird-cherry
        and yew-berries.

Resting there are herded swine,
        goats and piglings;
wild swine too, deer and doe,
        speckled badgers.

Great woodland bands troop like fairies
        to my bothy;
and great delight when timid foxes
        show their faces.

                *   *   *

Eggs in clutches and God gives mast,
        honey, heath-pease;
sweet the apples and the berries
        of bog and heather.

                *   *   *

Cúach meda colláin chunnla
    co ndáil daith;
durcháin donna, dristin monga
    mérthain maith.

Mad fri samrad suairc snobrat
    somlas mlas,
curair, orcáin, foltáin glaise,
    glaine glas.

Céola ferán mbruinne forglan
    foram ndil,
dordán smálcha caíne gnáthcha
    úas mo thig.

Tellinn, cíarainn, cerdán cruinne,
    crónán séim;
gigrainn, cadain, gair ré Samain
    seinm ngairb chéir.

        *   *   *

Tecat caínfinn, corra, faílinn,
    fos-cain cúan;
ní céol ndogra cerca odra
    a fráech rúad.

        *   *   *

Fogur gaíthe fri fid flescach
    forglas néol,
essa aba, esnad eala,
    álainn céol.

A cup of mead from noble hazel,
    swift the service;
acorns brown, bramble tresses
    and their berries.

Then in summer pleasant mantle
    of tasty savour;
marjoram, earth-nuts, and the tresses
    of the streamlet.

Pigeons cooing, breasts are gleaming,
    beloved flutter;
on my house-top constant music,
    song of thrushes.

Bees and chafers, gentle humming
    and soft crooning;
wild geese come with rough dark music
    before All Hallows.

*   *   *

Then come dear white ones, herons, sea-gulls
    sea-chant hearing;
no harsh music when grouse is calling
    from russet heather.

*   *   *

The sound of wind in branching trees,
    day grey and cloudy;
stream in torrent, swans are singing,
    sweet the music.

71

Caíne ailmi ardom-peitet,
    ní íarna creic,
do Chríst cech than ní messa daín
    oldás deit.

Cid maith lat-su a ndo-mil-siu,
    mó cach maín,
buidech lem-sa do-berr dam-sa
    óm Chríst chaín.

Cen úair n-augrai, cen deilm ndebtha
    immut foich,
buidech dond Fhlaith do-beir cach maith
    dom im boith.

XXVIII

Mé Éba

Mé Éba, ben Ádaim uill;
    mé ro-sáraig Ísu thall,
mé ro-thall nem ar mo chloinn,
    cóir is mé do-chóid 'sa crann.

Ropa lem rítheg dom réir,
    olc in míthoga rom-thár,
olc in cosc cinad rom-chrín,
    for-ír! ní hidan mo lám.

I hear the soughing of the pine-trees
        and pay no money;
I am richer far through Christ, my Lord,
        than ever you were.

Though you enjoy all you consume
        and wealth exceeding,
I am grateful for the riches
        my dear Christ brings me.

No hour of trouble like you endure,
        no din of combat:
I thank the Prince who so endows me
        in my bothy.

XXVIII

Eve

I am Eve, great Adam's wife,
because of me has Jesus died;
it were I, thief of my children's heaven,
by all rights were crucified.

I had a king's house to my wish,
but made an evil choice one day
that withered both my flesh and soul
and left my hand unclean this way.

Mé tuc in n-uball an-úas,
    do-chúaid tar cumang mo chraís;
in céin marat-sam re lá
    de ní scarat mná re baís.

Ní bíad eigred in cach dú,
    ní bíad geimred gáethmar glé,
ní bíad iffern, ní bíad brón,
    ní bíad óman minbad mé.

XXIX

A Chrínóc, Cubaid Do Cheól
MAEL ÍSU Ó BROLCHÁIN

A Chrínóc, cubaid do cheól,
    cenco bat fíróc at fíal;
ro-mósam túaid i tír Néill
    tan do-rónsam feis réid ríam.

Rop hí m'áes tan ro-foís lem,
    a bé níata in gáesa grinn,
daltán clíabglan cáem nád camm,
    maccán mall secht mbliadan mbinn.

Bámar for bith Banba bailc
    cen éilniud anma ná cuirp,
mo lí lasrach lán dot ṡeirc
    amail geilt cen aslach uilc.

Unclean! It snatched forbidden fruit
compulsively — it must, it must;
and hence forever, while women be,
live passion, folly, greed and lust.

There were no ice in any place,
there were no winter, no stormy sea,
there were no hell and no regrets,
there were no terror but for me.

XXIX

To An Old Psalm-book
MÁEL ÍSU Ó BROLCHÁIN

Crínóc, lady of measured melody,
    not young, but with modest maiden mind,
together once in Niall's northern land
    we slept, we two, as man and womankind.

You came and slept with me for that first time,
    (skilled wise amazon annihilating fears)
and I a fresh-faced boy, not bent as now,
    a gentle lad of seven melodious years.

There we were then on that firm Irish earth
    desirous, but in pure and mystic sense;
burning with love my flesh, still free from fault
    as fool of God in smitten innocence.

75

Erlam do chomairle chóir,
    dóig nos-togamne in cech tír
is ferr rográd dot gaeis géir,
    ar comrád réid frisin Ríg.

Ro-foís la cethrar íar sin
    im díaid cen nach methlad mer,
ro-fetar, is beóda in blad,
at glan cen pheccad fri fer.

Fo deóid dom rúachtais do-rís
    íar cúartaib scís, gleó co ngaeis;
do-dechaid temel tart gnúis,
    cen drúis is dered dot aeis.

At inmain lem-sa cen locht,
    rot-bía mo chen-sa cen cacht;
ní léicfe ar mbádud i péin,
    fo-gabam crábud léir lat.

Lán dot labrad in bith búan,
    adbal do rith tar cach rían;
día seichmis cech día do dán
    ro-seismis slán co Día ndían.

Do-beire do thimna in toí
    do chách co himda ar bith ché,
síthlai dúin uile in cech ló
    ní gó guide díchra Dé.

Your counsel is ever there to hand,
　　we choose it, following you in everything;
love of your word is the best of loves,
　　our gentle conversation with the King.

Guiltless you are of any sin with man,
　　fair is your name, and bright, and without stain,
although I know that when you went from me
　　　　each in his turn, four lay where I had lain.

And now you come, your final pilgrimage,
　　wearied with toil and travel, grimed with dust,
wise still but body not immaculate:
　　time it is that ravished you, not lust.

Again I offer you a faultless love,
　　a love unfettered for which surely we
will not be punished in the depths of hell
　　but together ever walk in piety.

Seeking the presence of elusive God
　　　　wandering we stray, but the way is found,
following the mighty melodies that with you
　　throughout the pathways of the world resound.

Not ever silent, you bring the word of God
　　to all who in the present world abide,
and then through you, through finest mesh,
　　Man's earnest prayer to God is purified.

77

Do-rata Día dellraid dúin
　　a ré frit ar menmain mín
rop rolainn frinn gnúis Ríg réil
　　íar n-ar léimm ór colainn chrín.

XXX

A Dhé, Tuc Dam Topur nDér

A Dhé, tuc dam topur ndér
　　do díl mo chinad, ní chél;
ní toirthech talam cen bráen,
　　ním náem cén anam cen dér.

XXXI

Mo Chinaid I Comláine

MAEL ÍSU Ó BROLCHÁIN

Mo chinaid i comláine,
　　in guth, in gním i cride,
rith mo rúathar rográinne
　　dílig dam, a Dé nime.

In tan ropsa móethóclach
　　ropsam dermatach dligid;
ba lainn lemm mo bóethphócad
　　do mnáib détgelaib dilib.

78

May the King give us beauty back again
    who ever did his will with quiet mind,
may he look on us with eagerness and love,
    our old and perished bodies left behind.

XXX

Tears

God, give me a well of tears
    my sins to hide,
or I am left like arid earth
    unsanctified.

XXXI

Confession
MÁEL ÍSU Ó BROLCHÁIN

Forgiveness, God, for all my sins
    I seek at last,
the sin in word, the deed in heart,
    foul sin compassed.

In heedless youth I broke the rule,
    made grievous slips,
offered fair women of gleaming teeth
    lascivious lips.

79

Tan atám ar senórach,
      íar cech thuitim co trúaige,
ní ferr lemm lá fledóla
      iná déra dar mo grúaide.

XXXII

Teicht Do Róim

Teicht do Róim,
      mór saído, becc torbai!
In rí chon-daigi hi foss,
manim-bera latt, ní fogbai.

XXXIII

Is Mo Chen In Maiten Bán

Is mo chen in maiten bán,
do-thét ar lár m'airiuclán,
is mo chen don tí rus-foí,
in maiten buadach bithnaí.

A ingen Aidche úaille,
a siúr na Gréine glúaire,
is mo chen, a maiten bán,
foillsiges orm mo lebrán.

Now I am an old, old man
    and after sinful years
I seek no feast but that my cheeks
    be wet with tears.

XXXII

Pilgrimage To Rome

Pilgrim, take care your journey's not in vain,
a hazard without profit, without gain;
the King you seek you'll find in Rome, it's true,
but only if he travels on the way with you.

XXXIII

Dawn

Come into my dark oratory,
    be welcome the bright morn,
and blessed He who sent you,
    victorious, self-renewing dawn.

Maiden of good family.
    Sun's sister, daughter of proud Night,
ever-welcome the fair morn
    that brings my mass-book light.

It-chí agaid cach tige,
soillsigi túaith is fine,
is mo chen, a muingel mass,
acainn, a órchaín amnass.

XXXIV

Ach, A Luin

Ach, a luin, is buide duit
    cáit 'sa muine i fuil do net,
a díthrebaig nád clinn cloc,
    is binn boc síthamail t'fet.

XXXV

Robad Mellach, A Meic Mo Dé

Robad mellach, a meic mo Dé,
    dingnaib réimenn
ascnam tar tuinn topur ndílenn
    dochum nÉirenn.

Co mag nEólairg, sech Beinn Foibne,
    tar Loch Febail,
airm i cluinfinn cuibdius cubaid
    ac na helaib.

Touching the face of each house,
    illumining every kin,
white-necked and gold-bedecked —
    welcome, imperious one. Come in.

XXXIV

The Blackbird

Blackbird, it is well for you
wherever in the thicket be your nest,
hermit that sounds no bell,
sweet, soft, fairylike is your note.

XXXV

Colum Cille's Exile

This were pleasant, O Son of God,
    with wondrous coursing
to sail across the swelling torrent
    back to Ireland.

To Eólarg's plain, past Benevanagh,
    across Loch Feval,
and there to hear the swans in chorus
    chanting music.

Sluag na Feblán robtis faíltig
    rér séol súntach,
día rísed Port na Ferg faíltech
    in Derg Drúchtach.

Rom-lín múich i n-ingnais Éirenn
    díamsa coimsech,
'san tír aineóil conam-tharla
    taideóir toirsech.

Trúag in turus do-breth form-sa,
    a rí rúine,
Ach, níma ndechad bu-déine
    do chath Chúile!

Ba ma-ngénar do mac Dímma
    'na chill chredlaig,
airm i cluinfinn tíar i nDurmaig
    — mian dom menmain —

fúaim na gaíthe frisin leman
    ardon-peite,
golgaire in luin léith co n-aite
    íar mbéim eite.

Éistecht co moch i Ros Grencha
    frisin damraid,
coicetal na cúach don fidbaid
    ar brúach samraid.

And when my boat, the Derg Drúchtach,
    at last made harbour
in Port na Ferg the joyful Foyle-folk
    would sound a welcome.

I ever long for the land of Ireland
    where I had power,
an exile now in midst of strangers,
    sad and tearful.

Woe that journey forced upon me,
    O King of Secrets;
would to God I'd never gone there,
    to Cooldrevne.

Well it is for son of Dímma
    in his cloister,
and happy I but were I hearing
    with him in Durrow

the wind that ever plays us music
    in the elm-trees,
and sudden cry of startled blackbird,
    wing a-beating.

And listen early in Ros Grencha
    to stags a-belling,
and when cuckoo, at brink of summer,
    joins in chorus.

Ro grádaiges íatha Éirenn,
    deilm cen ellach;
feis re Comgall, cúairt co Caindech
    robad mellach.

XXXVI

Fil Súil nGlais

Fil súil nglais
fégbas Éirinn dar a hais;
nocho n-aicceba íarmo-thá
firu Érenn nách a mná.

XXXVII

Tadhbhás Do Lugh, Leannán Teamhra
GOFRAIDH FIONN Ó DÁLAIGH

Tadhbhás do Lugh, leannán Teamhra,
    thoir i nEamhain,
dá ránaig sé ar súr gach domhain
    Múr Té, Teamhair.

Dúnta an chathair ar cionn Logha,
    laoch ro thoghsam;
téid gusan múr sleamhain slioschorr,
    beanaidh boschrann.

I have loved the land of Ireland
— I cry for parting;
to sleep at Comgall's, visit Canice,
this were pleasant.

XXXVI

The Backward Look

Grey eye there is
that backward looks and gazes;
never will it see again
Ireland's women, Ireland's men.

XXXVII

The Coming Of Lugh
GOFRAIDH FIONN Ó DÁLAIGH

East in Eamhain
Tara's lover, Lugh beheld
Té's fortress Tara
and leaving other lands he sought it.

He found the city closed before him,
our chosen hero;
against its portals, smooth and tapering
he strikes the hammer.

Ar an doirseóir ris an deaghlaoch
    fa doirbh ruaigfhearg:
'Cáit asa dtig an fear áith, ógard,
    bláith, geal, gruaiddearg.

Ris an doirseóir
adubhairt Lugh nár loc iomghuin:
'File meise a hEamhain Abhlaigh,
    ealaigh, iobhraigh.'

            *   *   *

Ar gcluinsin ar chan an macaomh,
    mór a thairm-séin,
d'agallaimh Thuath Dé don doirseóir,
    luath é ainnséin.

'Fear san doras', ar an doirseóir,
    'rén doirbh coimmeas,
an uile cheard ar a chommus,
    an dearg doinndeas'.

'Damadh é Lugh, leannán Fódla
    na bhfonn sriobhfhann
do bheith ann', ar Tuath Dé Danann,
    'dob é a ionam'.

'Geall n-éagaisg ón fhior san doras,
    damhna leisge,
nocho ndearnadh d'úir ná d'uisge
    dúil dán dleisde'.

Said the doorman to the hero,
     stout in combat:
'Whence comes the youth so tall and stalwart,
     smooth, bright, red-cheeked?'

To the doorman answered Lugh
     who feared no combat:
'A poet I from Appled Eamhain
     of swans and yew-trees.'

                    *   *   *

When he heard the youth's recital,
     great and famous,
haste he made to Danu's people
     with the message.

'A youth is coming,' said the doorman,
     'hard to match him.
All the arts are in his power,
     comely strong one.'

'Were it Lugh, the gentle-rivered
     Ireland's lover,
that were there,' said Danu's people,
     'it were timely.'

'To match in beauty him who stands there
     were cause for slowness,
no creature made of earth or water
     yet can dare it.'

89

'A thaobh, a aghaidh, a earla,
        eochair thogha,
triar ar snuadh aoil agus umha,
        agus fhola'.

    'Binne a theanga
ná téada meannchrot 'gá míndeilbh,
        ón sádhail suan,
i lámhaibh suadh agá sírsheinm'.

'Issé sin', ar sluag na cathrach,
        'ar gceann báidhe,
        aonmhac Eithne,
saorshlat ar nach beirthe báire'.

'Brosdaighthear', ar Tuath Dé Danann,
        'doirseóir Teamhra,
d'ionnsoighidh na craoibhe cubhra,
        aoighe Eamhna'.

XXXVIII

Athesc Findabrach

    Ba hed íarum athesc Findabrach,
    nach álaind at-chíd:
    ba háildiu lee
    Fróech do acsin tar dublind,

'His face, his hair, his body,
    key of choosing,
like blood and bronze, and lime for whiteness
    is the triad.'

'His tongue is sweeter
than lute-strings finely fashioned
    for gentle sleep
and ever played by expert fingers.'

'It is he,'
said Tara's people, 'our goal of loving,
    Eithne's lone son,
noble scion never conquered.'

'Doorman of Tara, let you hasten,'
    said Danu's people,
'to receive the branch of fragrance,
    guest from Eamhain.'

XXXVIII

Findabair Remembers Fróech

This, thereafter, is what Findabair used to say,
seeing anything beautiful:
it would be more beautiful for her
to see Fróech crossing the dark water,

in corp do rogili,
ocus in folt do roáilli,
ind aiged do chumtachtai,
int śúil do roglaissi,
is é móethóclách
cen locht, cen ainim,
co n-agaid focháel, forlethain,
is é díriuch dianim,
in chráeb cosnaib cáeraib dergaib
eter in mbrágait ocus in n-aigid ngil.
Is ed at-bered Findabair:
nícon acca ní
ro-sáissed leth
nó trian do chruth.

XXXIX

Eterne Deus

Eterne Deus,
duo sunt in Momonia
qui destruunt nos et bona nostra,
videlicet comes Ermonie
et comes Dessemonie
cum eorum sequacibus,
quos in fine destruet Dominus
per Christum Dominum nostrum.
Amen.

body for shining whiteness,
hair for loveliness,
face for shapeliness,
eye for blue-greyness,
a well-born youth
without fault or blemish,
face broad above, narrow below,
and he straight and perfect,
the branch with its red berries
between throat and white face.
This is what Findabair used to say:
She had never seen
anything a half
or a third as beautiful as he.

XXXIX

The Earls Of Ormond And Desmond

Eternal God,
there are two in Munster
who destroy us and what is ours.
These are the Earl of Ormond
and the Earl of Desmond
with those who follow them,
whom in the end the Lord will destroy
through Christ, our Lord.
Amen.

XL

An Droighneán Donn

Síleann céad fear gur léo féin mé
    nuair ólaim lionn,
is téann a dhá dtrian síos díom ag cuimhne
    ar do chomhrádh liom;
sneachta séidhte 's é dá shíor-chur
    ar sliabh Uí Fhloinn,
's tá mo ghrádh-sa mar bhláth na n-áirne
    ar an droighnéan donn.

XLI

Lughaidh, Tadhg Agus Tórna
FLAITHRÍ Ó MAOIL CHONAIRE

Lughaidh, Tadhg agus Tórna,
    ollaimh eólcha bhúr dtalaimh,
coin iad go n-iomad bhfeasa
    ag troid fán easair fhalaimh.

XL

The Blackthorn Bush

A hundred men think I am theirs
    when I drink wine;
but they go away when I start to think
    on your talk and mine.
Slieve O'Flynn is quiet, silent
    with snowdrift's hush,
and my love is like sloe-blossom
    on the blackthorn bush.

XLI

Irish Scholars
FLAITHRÍ Ó MAOIL CHONAIRE

Lughaidh, Tadhg and Tórna,
    your country's well-schooled lot,
what learned hounds they are
    fighting for an empty pot!

Notes to the Poems

An effort has been made to keep the following notes at a minimum, but at the same time sufficient references are generally given to enable the reader to follow the full textual history of any poem, other than modern folk-poetry. Where a poem has been edited and translated in Gerard Murphy's *Early Irish Lyrics* (EIL), reference has been made to that source rather than to any other. EIM refers to Murphy's *Early Irish Metrics* and *Bruchstücke* refers to Kuno Meyer's *Bruchstücke der älteren Lyrik Irlands*. Murphy's excellent work has been of inestimable value in the preparation of many of the texts in the present volume.

1. The Irish text of this poem was included in the ninth century *Vita Tripartita*. It also survived in a seventh century version translated into Latin by Muirchú moccu Machthéni. The Irish version dropped a line so that *canfaid míchrábud* of the present text is based upon *incantabit nefas* of Muirchú. The more archaic *tí* has been substituted for *bratt* of the Irish text. This emendation has been suggested by the alliterative principle upon which the poem is based and by the fact that the eighth century poet Blathmac son of Cú Brettan uses *tí chorcrae* of the purple cloak of the Passion. For *a méis*, 'from a table', of the present text, the Irish text has *a mias*, 'his table'. Muirchú has *a sua mensa*. The present edition is the first effort at reconstructing the original poem, which may well be sixth rather than seventh century. The poem is put in the mouth of a druidic opponent of St. Patrick, and is, of course, a satirical picture of a bishop saying Mass. It is important to remember that when this poem was written memories of paganism were by no means dead, and there was probably some hankering after the old ways. Note that I have translated *Amén, Amén*, as 'Be it thus. Be it thus'. Muirchú translated '*fiat, fiat*'. It seems to me that there is a pun in the original text: the congregation says

Amén, Amén, but the pagan listener hears the Irish words *Amin, Amin* 'Thus, thus' (?)

II-III.   Probably c.600 See *The Problem of St. Patrick* (Carney), pp.131-3.

IV.   Text from *Sancti Columbani Opera* (Walker), p.190.

V.   From Glosses on Augustine (Carlsruhe), *Thesaurus Paleohibernicus* (Stokes and Strachan), II, p.7. The editors failed to notice the metrical character of the piece. Poem XIII is a longer poem in the same metre.

VI.   See EIL, p.160. Dated by Murphy to the ninth or tenth century, but it is possibly earlier.

VII.   Extracts from *The Poems of Blathmac son of Cú Brettan* (Carney), Irish Texts Society, Vol. XLVII. See also *Old Ireland and Her Poetry* (Carney) in *Old Ireland*, ed. Robert McNally S.J. (1965). Blathmac lived in the middle of the eighth century.

VIII.   An extract from *Caoineadh na Maighdine,* a dramatic folk-prayer, still current. The present verses are as recorded by An Seabhac from the recital of Seán Bán O Conchobhair in 1902 (*An Seanchaidhe Muimhneach,* 1932, p.401).

IX, X.   From the St. Gall Priscian, *Thesaurus Paleohibernicus* (Stokes and Strachan) II, p.290. For IX see EIL., p.4. Ninth century.

XI.   See Kuno Meyer, *Four Old Irish Songs of Summer and Winter* (1903) p.18. Probably ninth century.

XII.   Attributed to the wife of Aed mac Ainmirech who was slain in 598. Probably eighth century. Meyer, *Bruchstücke,* 89.

XIII.   See Murphy EIL, p.82. In § 5 I have read *fírinne* for *fírithir,* assuming a mistranscription owing to *Cuirithir* in the preceding line.

XIV.   Ninth or tenth century. Meyer, *Bruchstücke,* 160, Murphy EIM, p.59.

XV.   Ninth century. See Murphy EIL, p.74. Here the quatrains corresponding to 27 and 35 of Murphy's text have been omitted. The text as given here differs in a number of important particulars from that of Murphy.

XVI.   Ninth or tenth century. See Meyer, *Bruchstücke*, 149, Murphy EIM, p.73.

XVII.   This poem, hitherto unpublished, is taken from National Library of Ireland Gaelic MS. I. The first quatrain is also found in Laud 610, the second in King's Inn MS. no. 12. In § 1 the MS. reads *in fót*, in § 4 *nochan fhuil*. The date would be about the eleventh or twelfth century, probably the former.

XVIII.   See *Eigse* II, pp.107-13.

XIX-XXIV.   About 845 Sedulius Scottus, with two companions, arrived on the continent, and was hospitably received by Hartgar, bishop of Liège, who made him *scholasticus* of the cathedral school, where he continued for about thirteen years. The text of the poems is as edited by Traube in *Poet. Lat. Car.* III. For an account of his life see the present writer's essay in *Old Ireland*, ed. Robert McNally S.J.

XXV.   Late tenth century. From Airbertach mac Coisse's lengthy geographical poem *Ro fessa hi curp domuin dúir*, Bodleian MS., Rawl. B 502, 77b.

XXVI.   See Murphy EIL, p.26. For the idea behind the poem see comment by the present writer in *Old Ireland*, ed. Robert McNally S.J., p.166.

XXVII.   See Murphy, EIL, p.10.

XXVIII.   See Murphy, EIL, p.50.

XXIX.   See my article *Eigse* IV, p.280. In the present text I have rejected a common emendation in § 2 of *a bé niata* to *a ben diatá*. The manuscript reading makes profound sense. The poet regards Crínóc as a warrior woman who undertakes the instruction of the young, as Scáthach did with Cú Chulainn.

XXX.   See *Eigse* I, p.248.

XXXI.   Eleventh century. From the Maynooth MS. 4a 10 10.

XXXII.   Ninth century. From the Codex Boernerianus, *Thesaurus Paleohibernicus* (Stokes and Strachan), II,p.296.

XXXIII.   See Mulchrone, *Caithréim Cellaig* (1933), p.13.

XXXIV.   Eleventh century (?). Meyer, *Bruchstücke*, 151.

XXXV.   Eleventh century. See Murphy, EIL, p.66.

XXXVI.   Eleventh century. See Murphy, EIL, p.64.

XXXVII.   c.1357. See E. Knott, *Irish Syllabic Poetry*, p.54.

XXXVIII.   Eighth century. See *Táin Bó Fraích* (M. Dillon), p.7.

XXXIX.   In 1381 Richard, bishop of Cloyne, celebrated a Mass in Dublin for the soul of Phillipa, the late Countess of March. He was charged that he 'did after beginning the accustomed preface introduce these words: *Eterne Deus* etc. and then omitted the divine words following but with a high voice said and sang these damnable words viz. *duo sunt, etc.*' The bishop was proceeded against for slander, schism and heresy and deprived of his see. See Edmund Curtis, *Calendar of Ormond Deeds*, II, p.168.

XL.   Folksong. See *Amhráin Mhuighe Seóla* (Mrs. Costelloe), p.72.

XLI.   Seventeenth century. See *Dánfhocail* (T. F O'Rahilly), p.31.

THE IRISH BARDIC POET

*A study in the relationship of Poet and Patron
as exemplified in the persons of
the poet, Eochaidh Ó hEoghusa (O'Hussey)
and his various patrons, mainly members of
the Maguire family of Fermanagh.*

*Given as the Statutory Public Lecture of the Celtic School
of the Dublin Institute for Advanced Studies*
20 March 1958

THE IRISH BARDIC POET

The Gaelic social order in Ireland lasted from centuries
before the beginnings of recorded history into the seven-
teenth century. It was in many ways an archaic society
the origins of whose institutions are to be sought in the
remote period of Indo-European unity. In this society the
composing of poetry was not the occupation of the
specially gifted, the aesthete, or the dilettante. Poetry,
even in Christian times, partook of the nature of a re-
ligious institution and was so closely woven into the fab-
ric of political Gaeldom that without it that society could
not continue to exist unless by changing its very essence.
This poetry of which I speak is the verse of praise or
blame which the official poet composed for a prince or
chief, and of which we have copious examples from the
earliest period of the literature down to the sixteenth
and seventeenth centuries when the Gaelic order finally
came to an end. Besides such poems we find in manu-
scripts the delightful personal lyrics which were first
popularised by Kuno Meyer in his *Ancient Irish Poetry*,
and of which I have recently published a collection.[1] Is
there any direct connection between these two types of
verse, or are we justified in completely dissociating the
occasional poem, the expression of personal feeling or
emotion, from the great mass of official verse which by its
very nature tends to be stylised, impersonal, and often—
let us admit it—quite insincere? Not merely are we not
justified in making such a dissociation, but it can even be

---

1 *Medieval Irish Lyrics* 1967, the first part of the present volume.

said that, without the firm supporting background of official verse, the more personal verse would never have come into being in the form in which it did; furthermore, that much of the personal verse was probably produced either by trained official poets in their leisure moments, or by that element in society, whether monastic or lay, that was constantly under their influence. The whole bardic order (which was the earliest trade union in Europe) over the centuries, or indeed the millennia, of its existence aimed at forging from the Irish language the finest instrument for their purpose that lay in its potentiality. The more personal poet had at his disposal the results of those centuries of experience and experiment, and it is this fact that makes Irish poetry, especially in the period 600-1100 A.D., one of the most interesting literary phenomena that Western Europe has to offer. We have not to do with a 'folk' poetry which has just come into being, but with the refined product of a literary class that had practiced its art for centuries. It is because of the existence of this class that, when Old Irish first comes into being as a literary language, we are not confronted with a dialect problem—if I may use a contradiction in terms, the 'literary' language had already been standardised in the pre-literary oral period.

Some years ago I set out to write a general essay on the early Irish poet. There was one question (indeed, amongst many) that I wished to answer. That is: when a poet was supported by a prince or chief, what would his attitude be to other princes and chiefs, and how far would he travel throughout the Gaelic world in the practice of his craft? Would for instance, a poet attached to the O'Donnells in Tír Conaill normally be expected to find his way, say, to Argyll or to Co. Kerry? There seemed to be no reason why not—indeed Senchán, the official poet of Guaire, the seventh-century king of Connacht, is shown in quite early material as visiting the Isle of Man, and there are suggestions that on occasion Irish poets at this period might practice their art even in parts of Britain other than the Gaelic areas of the island. As part of a general effort to deal with this question I decided to investigate the travelling of some official poet, a great number of whose poems had survived. I chose Eochaidh Ó hEoghusa (anglice Eochy O'Hosey), a sixteenth-century official poet, for the simple reason that so many of his poems had survived. In following his career, I became so interested in the man himself that, though material relevant to the original question came to light, the question itself faded into the background. I can do no better here than to give a brief account of his life: a picture of Eochaidh will in some measure be true of the more gifted of his profession down through the centuries, and will give some idea of the social and cultural background against which most of the surviving lyric poetry of Ireland was originally composed.

From about the year 1586 until after the battle of Kinsale in 1602 Eochaidh Ó hEoghusa held the position of ollav to three successive Maguires: Cú Chonnacht, Lord of Fermanagh, who died in 1589; his son, the famous Hugh, who was killed in 1600; and Cú Chonnacht Maguire, Hugh's half-brother, who fled with the Earls in 1607. Here it is my intention to show what we can learn of Eochaidh's relationship to the individual members of the Maguire family, especially Hugh, and to look briefly at his relationship to other lords and princes. But first it is necessary to state briefly what an ollav is.

An ollav is many things to a king or prince, but I would

say that he is most significantly the shadow of a high-ranking pagan priest or druid. When Ireland, somewhat later than 500 A.D., decided to regard itself as a fully Christian country a rather strange position arose. The druidic order had been the basis of Irish society, and that society could no more do without the druids than could we to-day abolish the civil service with a stroke of a pen. A compromise had to be arrived at: the druids became more or less Christian and the Christian church took over a certain number of their functions. But their organisation remained intact and an ollav in a given principality was accorded the status of a Christian bishop, or rather, to put matters in their proper order, a Christian bishop was given the status of a high-ranking druidic priest. Society had now become thoroughly schizophrenic and the prince stood there with an ecclesiastic on one side and an ollav on the other, both requiring grants of land and support. It is constant Irish tradition that a grave crisis arose in the middle of the sixth century, and this tradition must be accepted, though not in every detail, because such a crisis was economically inevitable. The difficulty in brief was this: the society which a hundred years earlier had supported one religion was now expected to support two. It appears that there was a widely held view that the poets should be completely suppressed. But the extreme course was avoided: instead the numbers of the poets were reduced, no doubt in rough proportion to the somewhat diminished services now required of them. The organisation of the poets and the church were obviously in some degree rivals, although it is incontestable that the poets produced men who, to judge by their verse, were as pious as any cleric. But despite natural rivalry. from the very beginning of Christianity in Ireland there

108

was a constant process of cross-fertilisation. Both organisations recruited their functionaries from the same class of society; it was not uncommon for a man who was a trained and practising poet to enter a monastery, and it also happened that monks sometimes reverted to lay life. However it be, in the earliest period of our written vernacular literature there was a large group of men who combined in themselves the native tradition and the new Christian learning. All our early literature is the result of this complexity, and, as I have stressed elsewhere, and continue to stress, there is no such thing (except perhaps in the more archaic law-tracts) as the pure native pagan element. In the medieval period certain families who sent their sons to be poets were families of no vast property, but of aristocratic ancestry. They were the upper middle-classes as distinct from the powerful land-owners. Judged according to Irish standards, Eochaidh Ó hEoghusa's ancestry was somewhat superior to that of the Maguires whom he served as ollav. The relationship of Eochaidh Ó hEoghusa to Hugh Maguire was essentially that of the sixth-century Dallán Forgaill to Aodh Fionn, the ancestor of the O'Rourkes and the O'Reillys, or that of the seventh-century Senchán to Guaire of Connacht. Going a little further back to the late fifth century we find Dubthach Moccu Lugair occupying an analogous position towards Crimthann, son of Énde Censelach, of Leinster; Dubthach was both poet and brehon and this perhaps suggests that the distinguishing of these two offices was not complete until the advent of Christianity. In the pre-Christian saga period Conor Mac Nessa's druid Cathbad is the figure who holds a post comparable with Eochaidh Ó hEoghusa's, and I might here mention that life in Fermanagh under the Maguires differed very little from the picture of life in

Ulster under Conor Mac Nessa; Hugh Maguire, in fact, was exactly the type of man who could have been built up in tradition into the figure of Cú Chulainn. One of the most famous of Irish poets was Rumann mac Colmáin who died about 747 and who had been ollav to the high-king Fergal, son of Mael Dúin, who was slain in 718. We can place Rumann's social and educational background very well. He was from the ecclesiastical town of Trim, was about twelfth in descent from King Laoghaire and his wife was of the same blood: he had, therefore, close on two and a half centuries of Christian ancestry. His brother was a bishop and two of his sons were abbatial successors in the monastery of Clonard. The Irish regarded Rumann as their equivalent of Virgil and Homer and for this and other reasons I am tempted to regard him as the man who first gave what we call its canonical form to Táin Bó Cuailnge: this work went through several editions and was undoubtedly used as a text book in the poetic schools, and occupied a central place in poetic thinking until the seventeenth century. Poets like Senchán, Rumann, and Eochaidh Ó hEoghusa were never story-tellers or entertainers: such a function would be very much beneath them. But they had to know Irish geneal-ogy, Irish history and pseudo-history: they had to know so many stories that no situation could arise in their pro-fessional career but they would have a convenient ana-logy from the past to apply to the present. Eochaidh Ó hEoghusa's exempla are drawn from Táin Bó Cuailnge, the history of Brian Bóroimhe and his sons, Lives of the Saints, Ovid, Lucan, medieval tales of European proven-ance, and from the history of the poetic order. I think we may safely say that he was thoroughly acquainted with the greater part of the literature that has survived in 14th and 15th century manuscripts: he must have read a considerable amount of Old Irish.

The poets of the 16th century knew themselves for what they were: successors of Athairne, Cathbad, Dallán, Senchán, and all the rest. This organisation preserved and propagated ideas on the nature of kingship and in these ideas we find our best relics of pre-Christian religion. A king married his territory: if he was effective and behaved as a king should, according to the ethical system of the poets, his land was fertile and bore fruit. If the king was bad, according to this ethical system, the land was barren. Practices of pagan origin lived on and in certain families it was an ollav who presided at an inauguration and who handed the prince the rod or wand which symbolised his mystic union with the land, with growth and fertility. Here the ollav is acting a part which is elsewhere played by a bishop: he is the intermediary between the prince and the mysterious powers of nature. Viewed in this light we can see why the satire of the poets was regarded with such awe. Satire in origin is a religious sanction and represents the means which the pagan 'church' used in order to exercise power over the state. If an ollav satirises a prince he is in effect telling him that the forces of nature, with which he, the ollav, is in communion, are not satisfied: the result of the satire is an injury to the king's honour (which may show physically as blisters on his face) and possibly a blight on the land. The converse of this necessarily holds: when a poet praises a king he is assuring him that the powers of nature find him pleasing and that the marriage is going well. Hence the poem of praise, as well as the satire, is in origin a religious act. There is a close and mystic bond between the prince and his ollav, and this may have

111

something to do with the fact that the ollav or druid was the prince's only possible approach to the earth goddess whose husband he was. This may explain the idea, basic to Irish thinking, that prince and ollav are in a symbolic sense husband and wife. Ó hEoghusa gives strong expression to what he regards as the legal right of the ollav to share the prince's bed and it is obviously a right upon which he sets considerable value. We must think of this in medieval, and not in modern terms: after a night's drinking, the whole company lay down where they could, and it was the poet's right and privilege to lie next to the prince. Such rights, we may assume, were guarded with some jealousy. Ireland became Christian but these ideas never died while the poetic order lasted. Hence in a treaty signed between Manus O'Donnell and O'Connor-Sligo in 1547 the satire of the poets and excommunication by the church are treated as equivalent sanctions: Irish society was still schizophrenic and was to remain so until Oliver Cromwell gave it its final death-blow.

The history of the poetic order has not been written, but certainly in the thirteenth century there were at least rumours that it was to be condemned at Rome. This did not happen, however, and about 1580, although its ruin was imminent, the poets were as strong in certain areas as they had ever been since the introduction of Christianity. What has been lacking until now we can find in Ó hEoghusa: some of the personal history of a traditional Irish ollav and his place in the society which supported him. He is a figure from whom we can generalise, to some extent even for the dim pre-Christian period for which contemporary evidence is totally lacking. But before touching on his personal history there is one point which must be made. Eochaidh considered his relationship to Hugh Maguire as a marriage. This idea I have already referred to and it can be traced in Ireland from the seventh century to the seventeenth, and there is hardly the slightest doubt but that it is part of the poetic order's pre-Christian inheritance. This is an idea to which Eochaidh is more addicted than any other poet I know. He seems to have lived his whole life according to it, to have geared all his emotions to it, and he constitutes its most extreme expression.

This, I must emphasise, was a conceit. I first came upon this conceit in the matter of the well-known and much discussed poem *Féuch féin an obair-se, a Aodh*, to which I devoted a chapter in my *Studies in Irish Literature and History*. This poem, it was thought, expressed the distraction of Aodh O'Ruairc's wife when she found herself torn emotionally between her husband and her lover, Thomas Costelloe. But it has been possible to show that there was, in fact, no wife involved. There was only the dilemma of the poet, probably one Tomás Ó hUiginn, who found it impossible to know whether he should give his best love to O'Ruairc or to Costelloe. When I first wrote upon this matter I had not realised how widespread was this conceit in bardic thinking. Its effect was this: that such language could be used to a patron, that the resulting poem could pass for an expression of the deepest passion. I would suggest *en passant* that English scholars should give some thought to the fact that Irish poetry of this type would offer a very plausible model for the language and attitudes that we find in Shakespeare's sonnets.

The first approach to a biography of Eochaidh Ó hEoghusa is to read his poems; about fifty survive and fully half of them are unpublished and must be read in manuscript. The next problem is to get them into an approximate chronological sequence and in this we are helped by having regard to the history of the person addressed. Sometimes, indeed, we can narrow a poem down to a month. Eochaidh leaves us one very important clue. In the very beginning of his career he made a bargain with Hugh that whatever praise-poem he would write he would always include a quatrain to him, and the surviving poems show that he invariably, or almost invariably, kept this bargain. Poems which speak of Hugh in the present tense may be taken as before 1600. Poems speaking of him in the past tense are generally between 1600 and 1603. After the death of Red Hugh O'Donnell in Spain, Eochaidh commemorates not Hugh Maguire alone but *an dá Aodh do imthigh uaim*, 'the two Hughs who left me'. In all this matter Hugh is of course silent and our main witness is Eochaidh. But even apart from Eochaidh's evidence it is quite clear that Hugh's was the type of personality that attracted and inspired. Sir John Davies said that he was 'a valiant rebel and the stoutest that ever was of his name'. He and his brother Cú Chonnacht, Davies tells us, were the Alpha and the Omega of the rebellion: Hugh was the first of the Irish to come out and Cú Chonnacht was the last to come in. Elizabeth took heart when she heard of Hugh's death which was the first good news she had had from Ireland for a long time; indeed, for the Irish his death may be regarded as marking the beginning of the end. The most picturesque suggestion of Hugh's personal attractiveness is given in a poem by Tadhg Dall Ó hUiginn in which he contrasts him with his father, Cú Chonnacht. Hugh is so popular, Tadhg Dall tells us, that it is no use competing for his company: he leaves him to the nobles and poets who surround him and goes to his father Maguire, the whole of Maguire being better than the little of Hugh that he would get by entering into competition with the rest. As an analogy he tells us how seventeen Connacht poets had a pig and an ox cooked for them. Each in turn was asked which meat he would have and, in accordance with the well-known Irish preference, sixteen declared for the pork and one was left to dine off the beef. Tadhg Dall would prefer Maguire, the whole ox, to sharing Hugh with the rest.

It is at such a party, probably held at Enniskillen Castle about the year 1586, that we meet Eochaidh and Hugh together for the first time. Hugh was a young man at the time and Eochaidh a mere student; the latter would probably have been no more than eighteen, which would place his birth about 1568. As in Tadhg Dall's poem Hugh is the centre of a convivial group who are drinking ale and discussing poetry. One of the company on request recited a poem which a Munster poet, Gofraidh Fionn Ó Dálaigh (author of poem xxxvii in my *Medieval Irish Lyrics*), had made about two centuries before to a Northern prince. In this poem Gofraidh Fionn had included a single quatrain in praise of O'Brien of Thomond. Hugh was curious about this, or affected to be curious. 'Poets,' he asked, 'why did Ó Dálaigh make the quatrain for the Munster prince. Was it a sign of love?' Eochaidh was the one to answer and said that it was not because of his love for Conor O'Brien, but that O'Brien used to give Gofraidh a horse every year for this single-quatrain concession. In other words, it was strictly a business arrangement: O'Brien wanted publicity and Gofraidh Fionn, amongst other things, was an advertising agent. When Hugh heard this, Eochaidh tells us, he had a great wish for the same thing. He turned to Eochaidh and said: 'Why haven't you made an arrangement with me like they had?' Eochaidh replied that he would rather make that bargain with Hugh than with any of the nobles of Ireland. The poem where Eochaidh describes this incident was written for Hugh as a record of the bargain. In a glow of fervour and enthusiasm he ends with the words: 'This bargain I have made with the heir to the palace of the Boyne, my verse will give effect to it in a way that will be no shame to him or to me. Jesus willing, you of the soft hair, it will seem dastardly to both of us if we ever hurt each other. O Hugh, welcome to your bargain.'

Sometime after this a new, and perhaps unexpected situation arose. The ollavship to Maguire was vacant. I have already stressed what an important post this was, and although in Irish law the ollav was the social equivalent of a bishop, in fact, in this time and place he was obviously much more important. He would be ambassador, spy, 'native-bishop', chief counsellor, genealogist, official praiser of the prince, and he should infuse all these activities with what the Irish as early as the eighth century had learnt to call the spirit of poetry. In 1585-6 Eochaidh was, as I have said, still an unfinished poet, and he was living at the family home in Ballyhosey. He had two advantages to outweigh his youth and inexperience: he was from a local poetic family with a long traditional connection with the Maguires and he was friendly with Hugh. There may have been many applicants for the post, but we know from a poem in the Maguire *duanaire* in Copenhagen that about this time a Conor Ó Dálaigh from Munster sought to become ollav to Maguire. Munster in the early 1580's had suffered war and confiscation. Ó Dálaigh, to use his own terms, had been 'lover-poet' to three great Geraldines: Gerald, Earl of Desmond, the romantic James Fitzmaurice, and Sir John of Desmond.

By 1583 all had been slain and now he sought Maguire as his fourth spouse. That three of his successive patrons had come to a tragic end was hardly the best possible recommendation and Eochaidh, as yet not fully qualified as a poet, was raised to the rank of ollav.

If this were a play the unfortunate poet from Munster would be an important minor figure. Eochaidh, a talented and worldly-wise boy, has pushed himself up to what amounts to an episcopal dignity: the whole world seems to lie at his feet and he is set fair to attain to the summit of dignity to which the Irish social order could admit him. His success is underlined by the contrasting figure of the ruined Ó Dálaigh whose great world has suddenly and unexpectedly collapsed. But not merely does Ó Dálaigh contrast with Eochaidh, but by a curious dramatic irony, he is almost an exact mirroring of his future. Before many years had passed Eochaidh was also to lose three men to whom he was deeply devoted: Hugh, his 'first spouse', his 'sweetheart', was to be killed; Cú Chonnacht was to be exiled and to die of fever in Italy, while Red Hugh O'Donnell was to die of poison in Spain. In addition Eochaidh in his short life was to outlive practically every powerful man who had ever shown him favour; he was to taste the bitterness of knowing that society no longer valued the only thing he knew, the art and profession for which he was not merely trained, but actually predestined and born.

But meanwhile things could hardly be better, although Eochaidh, feeling his own inadequacy, shirked for a time his first duty which was to praise old Maguire. Finally, however, the night came when he had his first poem ready. Maguire is credited with a scholarly knowledge of Irish and Latin and was probably a formidable critic.

Whatever he thought of Eochaidh's first poem, to me it reads like what one would expect: a mixture of nervousness and youthful brashness. It also shows what we have already seen: Eochaidh's interest in property. We also see him in the strange position of being ollav to one man, and including in his poem, in fulfilment of his bargain, a quatrain in praise of another.

He begins: 'Now I shall praise Maguire.' Then with a facility which was to grow with the years he produces a situation from the past to illustrate the present. Enrí, son of Eoghan Ó Néill, he tells us, had as a poet and only lover Brian Ruadh Mac Con Midhe. It was not Brian's fault but he was really too young to be Ó Néill's poet so he refused to make a poem for him until he felt himself ready. Then finally he came forward with a praise-poem in which he showed full mastery of his craft. That night Ó Néill rewarded him with affection that was excessive for a poet, and ever afterwards he used to get whatever he wished in the way of lands and riches. The same position, Eochaidh points out, has now arisen. He has been a long time without composing a poem for Maguire; he has in fact been learning his craft while with Maguire, and now at last he is ready. Towards the end of the poem, before giving his duty quatrains to Maguire's wife, he turns to Hugh:

> I promised Hugh of the merry mind
> a *rann* in every poem I'd make;
> fair soft hand that took my love,
> there is no fear I'll change from him.

Maguire died in 1589 and Hugh, not without difficulty, and requiring the support of his first cousin O'Donnell, father of Red Hugh, succeeded to the lordship of Fermanagh. Many of Eochaidh's poems have an intensely personal quality: unlike the average professional product his praise-poems tend towards subjectivity. But this subjectivity is lacking in his inauguration ode and his eventual elegy on Hugh. He gives what the occasion demands, and he gives it with vigour, grace and a measure of originality. His inauguration poem is, of course, for a state occasion and for the first time we see him venturing into high politics:

'Ireland is in the mood for love and has put on her wonderful raiment of green and purple and gold. The voices of her streams are low and she is wooing Hugh who is the second Naoise of the Ulstermen. It is for him she has put on her wonderful clothes and cast aside her mourning and enchantment.

There was once a youth of the Greeks who, having become a knight, set out on a journey; he came to a stream in a dark and gloomy glen where he found a disfigured maiden weeping. He asked her the cause of her misery and how he could help her. Once, she said, she was a happy maiden, merry and wise, and had many suitors. One day with her maids she went to bathe and a terrible bewitching shower fell from the heavens and left her in the condition in which he found her. The philosophers prophesied that a fine youth of angelic aspect would come: he would wash her in the stream and she would be released from her misery. The knight fulfilled the prophecy and thereupon her countenance became as a mixture of the whiteness of a swan and the redness of Parthian leather. He loved her and they married. Ireland is the maiden, the bewitching shower was the English, and the stream in which Hugh will wash Ireland is their blood. Hugh Maguire will make a modest woman of the old wife of Conn Céadchathach and the ideal kingdom of peace and prosperity will return as in the days of Conn and Conaire. Hugh's is the hand that protects Fermanagh; he is a frozen sea against the O'Neills and he is a stone wall against the O'Donnells. Hugh can unite Ireland.'

Towards the end of this poem Eochaidh seems to have got somewhat entangled in the web of his own making. His vision of Hugh as king of Ireland is something which neither poet nor patron would take very seriously. Hugh as a stone wall against the O'Donnells is particularly inappropriate seeing that he is half an O'Donnell by blood and has just become Lord of Fermanagh by the grace and favour of his O'Donnell cousin. Similarly when he is a frozen sea against the O'Neills we must remember that his step-mother, the mother of his brother and successor Cú Chonnacht, is an O'Neill. And, of course, being a frozen sea against one great Irish family and a stone wall against another is hardly the best way to promote the union of Ireland which Eochaidh envisages. In a poem like this Eochaidh is simply doing the done thing, and nothing more and nothing less is expected of him. It is the type of poem which was just beginning to degenerate into the *Aisling* (Vision) which is so well-known from the Munster poets of the succeeding centuries.

It is certain that Eochaidh took his art very seriously. He was conscious of defects and of a certain degree of ignorance and he decided, apparently with no enthusiasm on Hugh's part, to go to Munster — where exactly in the province we do not know — for further study. From Munster he wrote to Hugh the poem *Atáim i gcás idir dhá chomhairle,* 'I am in a dilemma between two counsels.' In complete contrast with the last poem we have seen, which was for public utterance on a state occasion, this poem, like many others, must be treated as a personal letter. I shall treat it as such, giving a partial abstract, cutting out many of the words and phrases that have no purpose other than to fulfil the demands of a particularly complicated metre:

'I am in a dilemma between two counsels, two opposing forces of equal magnitude which effectively impede all action. On the one hand there is the love of learning, as it were fosterage, and on the other my desire to remain in the North, the mother who bore me. Sometimes in my depression I think that I shall return with my work unfinished and when I am about to set out to you I think that it is not wise to leave having gone the first step on the ladder. I shall stay until the end on small resources. But how hard it is! Yet if I stay away from the North is it not right that a king-poet should travel every territory? But I will not leave the North a second year. Even were they to give me here their companionship, the sharing of their kingly pillows, and reward greater than others, still in my exile from the melodious assembly of Fermanagh, the thought of seeing them again would be like a healing herb. Sad was my coming to Munster, and though Munster is dear to me, I do not like it that my lover is displeased. Alas, my travelling from the North, from the beautiful Erne, from the Maguires and the people of Fermanagh, and from my own Hugh, spouse of guests and protection of shepherds, whom I love more than any of the Irish. It is my hope that my visit away from my only spouse of his great race will not be long, from the Maguire to whose kingly palace I shall come, slender-handed fairy from the palace of the Boyne. In that beautiful fairy palace of Hugh, my body's defending girdle, my invigorating ale, and without travelling from that lime-white palace, I shall have vision of every delight in Ireland.'

There follow some stanzas which are a further anticipation of the delights of life in Fermanagh and he ends with an apostrophe of Hugh: 'My darling spouse, beloved of every visitor, he who causes the poets of Ireland to labour, he who gilds our art more than the best in this western land. Welcome fair head with hair like heavy bending forest to whom I shall give companionship during a long journey. And the fine pure-white breast, the pillow on which I rest, the refreshing of my mind.'

Possibly Eochaidh was unwise to leave Hugh for so long. In terms of the conceit which governs the expression of this whole situation the honeymoon is over and the economic factor becomes dominant; also true to pattern other women enter the situation, but the female parts are, of course, played by poets, and there is one in particular of whom Eochaidh is jealous. Hugh's life as Lord of Fermanagh can be divided into two parts. From 1584 to 1592 he was at peace; from 1593 to 1600 he was at war. The period of peace was a time of gaiety and it would seem that within this period there was a minimum of a year and a half during which he was cold towards Eochaidh.

Eochaidh was now *ex officio* an important man and had, of course, to have an establishment. Hugh had given him a stocked farm at a place called Corrán in the barony of Lurg, about nine miles from Enniskillen. From here Eochaidh writes three poems in which he criticises Hugh vigorously, and these three poems are probably part of a longer series, for he could be quite voluble about his wrongs. The order in which I put the poems is tentative. In what I regard as the first poem Eochaidh complains about his land. It is situated on the confines of Fermanagh and he has to endure the opposition of the neighbours who thwart him in every way. Hugh's gifts are valueless if he suffers them to be seized. They, the neighbours, accuse him of not cultivating this land, which but yesterday was the habitation of wolves. But even if these people accepted him he would not wish to remain. It is a spot where four roads meet and is exposed to raiders; his profit from the land is not equal to half the losses he has suffered. But even if the O'Neills and O'Donnells represent no threat, the neighbours who are a branch of the Maguires are in league with Hugh's own unjust stewards. He must have land close to Hugh where he will have his protection. Furthermore when the harsh weather comes his stock will die. But why should he worry? It will be Hugh's duty to replace them.

In this *démarche* Eochaidh's complaints are limited and specific: bad land, local opposition, lack of protection. Apparently not only did Hugh not accede to his demand but he gave Eochaidh such further cause for complaint that he is forced to write a long and valuable poem on the rights and privileges of an ollav. In this poem he claims the right to be what we might call Prime Minister of Fermanagh:

'The title 'prince's ollav' is one of great dignity, and though art is itself honourable, a man who holds that title is due respect even above that which belongs to his art. Even if an ollav is unlearned he must be respected on account of the king who has ordained him. King, bishop, and ollav are the three noblest titles: they have the same *éric*, the same honour-price, and they are entitled to the same affection and protection. A king has nothing greater in his bestowal than the title of ollav. But alas for him who gets this title and its profits if the affection in which he is held is lessened! An ollav is entitled to the deepest affection, the best of presents, and must be first in counsel. He is to be at the prince's shoulder, to share his bed and get retribution for any loss, or for any failure in protection. He is to be chosen to act when peace is being made and is to enter into contracts with neighbouring territories. All this is due to me and if I do not obtain it, it reflects upon you. It is not right for me or for you, Hugh Maguire, that I should be in envy of one like myself. Admit this. I have discharged all my obligations. I have had the best training in Ulster and Munster and am a veritable bee in learning. I ask nothing that is not justified by precedent and I seek to change no law. If I am discontented the fault is yours and I am glad I am not open to reproach. No one should precede me in your counsel, there should be no power over me — else, repudiate me as your ollav. You, if you behaved properly, should ward off numerous tribes to do me honour, you should plunder other people at my behest. I am also entitled to a quiet estate in perpetuity, rent free, except for the best I can give in the way of art. All your wealth and plunder is of no use to me without land to keep stock: land is the imperishable wealth. We poets all seek land beside a prince, with both grazing and tillage, and to leave the wild mountain border-land. This you can do: give me possession of an estate beside your own dwelling which will not be a mark for raiders. If you think it is no loss to you that I am far away from you in time of council-meetings, then can I endure the envy and harshness that I must bear living in an outlying border territory. It is one of the ollav's duties to be close to the prince's dwelling: a king needs a knowledgeable guiding rudder. There are precedents: Conor Mac Nessa gave his poet Dungannon, Corc of Cashel gave Torna the place called Puball Pádraig, Maol Seachluinn gave Iorard Mac Coise Cláirtheach, Brian mac Cinnéide gave Aitheas Ó Lorcán seven townlands in addition to what he asked for. None of these poets got any affection which I do not expect from you. If I am not worth it, why do you not do it for the sake of your honour? Even if I were without poetic eloquence your great honour has ennobled me. My honour is yours, yours is mine, your strength is my strength, your prosperity is mine; injury to me is an injury to you and my advancement is an enhancing of your power.'

At this point Eochaidh shows that he is jealous of other poets and of one in particular. He has already hinted at this. His remarks are not completely intelligible because we do not know the full situation. 'They who welcome me,' he says 'are not those who honour me in speech. Though the person I mention be worthy, it is not he who threw at me what was thrown. Not him alone have you enlarged, Hugh Maguire, but many poets besides. It is your due that you own the whole poetic order. What they have got from you leaves them no cause for complaint — the hurley-match has gone to one side.'

He ends the poem with a series of complimentary epithets, interspersed with a few that are satirical: 'O plundering of the virginity of a woman,' 'O instrument of the implementing of an evil law,' 'O ward of a robber castle,' 'O breaking of the word of a prince.'

In the third poem, in which Eochaidh mentions the period of a year and a half, he starts so gently that at first we seem to be dealing with a praise-poem. Satire destroys the king's honour (*ainech*): figuratively speaking it raises blisters on his face, and, of course, the Irish words for "face" and "honour" are identical. Eochaidh speaks as if verses of poetry were arrows which remained in the body of a prince. He wishes to praise Hugh, but he has been praised so much by other poets that there is no vacant spot on his body to which he can direct his arrows. Hugh's house is a place of assembly for the poets of Ireland and they have made a pillow of him. He then tells one of his little stories to illustrate the situation.

'There was a knight long ago and when he fared forth, leaving his castle undefended, it was taken by enemies. These men, one after the other lay with the knight's wife. Finally there came to her the knight's page who spoke and said: "I will not spare you, woman, since I see you with everybody." You are that woman: here in the North you are a harlot amongst a multitude and wish to refuse nobody. I· am that page. I regret what I have let you go with, you harlot, Maguire: you have entertained the *tromdhámh* (the heavy-guesting) of Irish poets. For a year and a half I have got nothing from you while there is hardly a poet in Ireland who has not had presents even in the space of a year.'

In 1593 a new period begins in Hugh's life. He was, as has been said, the Alpha of the nine years war; to borrow other words he had become 'a man of action as rebels are called in this kingdom.' Eochaidh was clearly anti-English, and saw the threat they offered to the whole Gaelic way of life. What Hugh was doing was surely right and just. But Eochaidh was cautious and in a poem he tells him the story of the thirty philosophers whose wisdom was tantamount to madness. The moral of this

126

poem is: eat well, drink well, and sleep comfortably; the rest of the Irish are passive fools, and Hugh is actively wise; but being odd-man-out makes him in fact the fool.

There are so many of Eochaidh's poems extant for the decade following 1595 that it would be impossible to deal with them in any fullness. There are poems to Red Hugh whom Eochaidh had admired when he was but a student and when Red Hugh was not yet fifteen; to Rory O'Donnell, Hugh O'Neill, McSweeney, McMahon, O'Byrne, Rose O'Toole, O'Rourke, Tibbot Burke, Ulick Burke. Most of these poems contain a reference to Hugh, in fulfilment of the old bargain, and whatever their domestic differences, Eochaidh always presents Hugh to the outside world as the ideal prince. These poems of Eochaidh are not always mere praise-poems. He speaks as one important man to another and there is often advice which amounts to criticism. We have three poems of his to Conor McDermot of Sligo who had become an ally of Red Hugh, hence of Hugh Maguire. In 1595, together with Red Hugh, he had attacked many castles in Connacht, and Red Hugh, in accordance with his general policy, had him made captain of his people. Eochaidh's poems to him are a mixture of praise and criticism. The fatherland is being ruined by the mutual enmity of the Irish and the Old English. Connacht was very ill; McDermot has been her doctor and he has earned the leeching fee which he has now received; he has cauterised her and administered a bitter draught which should lead to health. Eochaidh, always interested in property, points out that reconstruction of the ruined castles will be necessary: 'Your bright countenance,' he says, 'will have great trouble when it comes to putting the stones back in their places.' He recommends more wine, more conviviality as a means of absorbing

127

dangerous, if patriotic, energies. This is essentially the advice he has given to Hugh. McDermot did not remain consistently loyal to Red Hugh; he joined the English for a while and had to be coaxed or forced back into the alliance. About March 1600 Eochaidh addressed a curious poem to him: he has heard from gossip that McDermot is displeased with him, and he points out that there is no real reason for anger. Poets have always been hard on princes and all McDermot's ancestors have suffered in this way. He should not pursue enmity with him; indeed it appears to Eochaidh that he is merely affecting anger in order to elicit praise. He, Eochaidh, is a dangerous opponent and has the support of Hugh Maguire. McDermot should act like Hugh, who was never really angry with him. When Eochaidh had finished this poem news came of Hugh's death and he appended a bitter and insulting quatrain. He says in effect: 'You may take me if you like — I am widowed. When Hugh was alive you had no chance.'

Possibly it was in the period 1595-1600 that Eochaidh visited Sir Seán O'Doherty of Inishowen, a cousin of Hugh Maguire's. There are two poems extant from Eochaidh to O'Doherty; the first is a formal poem of praise; the second is written from Fermanagh after his return. It was doubtless sent by messenger as a 'thank-you' letter, and it shows Eochaidh's genuine appreciation of O'Doherty, and how in odd quarters of Ireland life could go on in a very pleasant manner despite the war:

'Alas for him who leaves the faces of friends whether they are long or short together — it is not the best thing that those who are dear to each other should be together for but a short time. Who, however hard of heart, will leave those he loves without his heart being full of sorrow? This has happened to me. O'Doherty has smothered my mind with grief; my misery of mind is the measure of my love for his slim gentle body and for the time I spent with him. I have never had, nor shall I have, the like of the pleasure I had with O'Doherty. My visit to him was like the visit of Conghal Cinn Maghair across the sea with Ábhartach, the journey of Cormac mac Airt to the land of promise, or the expedition of Criomhthann Nia Náir when he got the treasures. Mongán in his long stay with Manannán can have had no greater joy; nor did Fionn, looking from the fairy mountain of the Fir Feimhin, see any sight that I did not see in that western land. Wonderfully did I spend my time: a day listening to harp-music, a day hunting in the bordering mountains, a day solving riddles and putting them in the company of guests and young women; sporting in the breasts of mountains, drinking, playing chess, out along the coast in sailing boats. We used to see as far as Cantire and to the borders of Ulster from the moist sloping breasts of purple peaks: I was enchanted by this exotic pleasure. Every consideration, every honour that I got, I pay for it with excessive despair. I resemble Brendan who in his loneliness was visited by a bird of wondrous melody. Brendan had gone to seek a solitude and one day there came to him a bird, whose chanting was more marvellous than any music. The bird was the archangel Michael who had been sent from heaven to keep Brendan company in his solitude. After some time the bird went away. Brendan mourned it for seven years so that when he heard any music he put two balls of wax in his ears. O'Doherty, I am like Brendan from the time of honour and pleasure you gave me. I smother the light of my heart, I close the doors of my love: no love suffices. Since I left you my mind is covered with a cloak of despair, even though I am in the land where I was reared. Every glory, every honour that I got from you, has left me in confusion and misery. . . . Those who lose their torch on a dark night are blind. He who has been happy and wealthy cannot bear to be poor. So it is with me: my misery is the greater for the pleasure I have known with you. Sweet loved one, you have found some means to warm me towards you, or you have magical charms. My love for you is not because I am half ollav to you: your directness of mind, your pleasantness, your gentleness, your youth have enchanted me. Your kindly gifts and your love have beguiled me in a way I did not expect. I have no regret that I am beguiled like the women of Ireland — I part not from effeminacy, O bright-coloured garnered ear of corn.

Another man beguiled me, Maguire of the fairy-like weapons; he beguiled me, and I him.

There follow three stanzas in praise of O'Doherty's wife who is apparently a daughter of Shane O'Neill.

We now move on to the winter of 1600. Hugh has gone to Munster to support O'Neill and Eochaidh stays in Fermanagh and worries. On some cold night probably in February of that year Eochaidh wrote the poem which is best known from Mangan's adaptation which begins:

Where is my chief, my master, this bleak night *mavrone!*
O, cold, miserably cold is this bleak night for Hugh,
Its showery, arrowy, speary sleet pierceth one through and through,
Pierceth one to the very bone.

Mangan has, of course, MacPhersonised Eochaidh, but

much of the original comes through. The poem is subjective, has no eulogistic purpose, and is compassion in the literal sense. I shall not attempt any summary of this poem. For my present purpose, which is mainly historical, it is sufficient to point out that Eochaidh expresses his fear for Hugh but, as if superstitiously, avoids explicit mention of his death: 'May I not regret, nor he, his journey around Ireland. The fear that seizes me, may it pass by. May my ruin not come.'

But Eochaidh's fears were justified, and Hugh was killed in Co. Cork in the month of March in an encounter with Sir Warham St. Leger.

Eochaidh's elegy on Hugh lacks the personal note and was no doubt composed for formal public recitation. The poem consists of eighty-seven stanzas and I can at the moment only indicate its nature briefly. It is Ireland's consistent fate, Eochaidh says, that those who try to save her are struck down. Whenever her illness was on the point of being cured, fate inflicted upon her a savage wound, and it was all too easy for Eochaidh to sustain this pessimistic thesis by examples from Ireland's past. But then he comes to a highly interesting and optimistic comparision. Hugh is the Pelican, the bird that gives its life's blood to revive its young who have been slain by the serpents. Hugh's blood is a draught which will revive the descendants of Conn. Eochaidh would naturally have been acquainted with the fact that the Pelican is a well-known symbol of Christ. His comparison amounts to a comparison of Hugh with Christ and is apparently the first nationalistic application of the idea of redemption through bloodsacrifice. Eochaidh ends with a *caithréim*, or list of Hugh's victories in battle.

Somewhat over a year later the Spaniards have landed

at Kinsale and Cú Chonnacht Maguire, now Lord of Fermanagh, sets out to join them. Eochaidh makes a poem to the Maguire standard and keeps his promise to Hugh by adding as the final stanza: 'Many a territory did you go around, O standard of Hugh Maguire, who now lies in a heavy sleep in Cork.'

From a poem written some two months later we can reconstruct some of Eochaidh's part in this affair. He set out with Cú Chonnacht but he was apparently wounded in a skirmish and persuaded to return to Fermanagh. His wounds were not yet healed fifty-two days later. Cú Chonnacht, it would seem, thinking that he must be well, had sent a message to Fermanagh asking Eochaidh to join him. Eochaidh's poem, written one night in his sick bed, explains to Cú Chonnacht that he cannot come. Again I give an abstract:

'The vision of my mind looks far. Alas it has made me an exile that my whole vision does not bring me into the sight of my beloved. That sight that would be joy for me, that voice that would beguile me, that they are far away has blinded the vision of my mind. I lie sick with mortal wounds for two months past: it seems long until I see that herb that would cure me. Maguire's journey around Ireland has worn me down with anguish: alas, I shall be sick until Cú Chonnacht Maguire returns. To-night from me in Ulster my spouse is far away amidst a wattling of spears in the very west of Ireland. It is not likely that I shall live here in Ulster when my soul is in Munster. Since Maguire went away no day passes and the days that have gone are still before me. I cannot ask tidings of him on account of my fears; I willingly remain in uncertainty, never hearing any news; I hear no two people whisper but my heart jumps; no news is told but I am terrified before I get to the bottom of it. What terrible captivity to be without him for fifty-two days when even one day is long without him. I would not be as I am, and I would not have such fear for him, if I were near him: if I experienced the terror that he experiences it would cool the fever of my mind. Not alone for enemies do I fear, though there are spears before him in every path; I fear more the dark beast of the winter night attacking him with her weapon and every bleak rough winter's morning. But it would be no misery for me to be with him in his plight, the elements piercing my body in a bare house under the same quilt as Cú Chonnacht. I would not complain of the constant wind through the opening of the tents or the rain beside my bed if in the evil weather I were with him. Beside Cú Chonnacht I would feel no anguish or evil; if he and I shared a bed I would heed no hardship. The cabins would be palaces, the cold streams would be wine, the earthen pillows would be soft down beside the descendant of Conn. Pitiful for me to remain away from him — I did not stay through my wish, but I suffered myself to be sent back. Whatever bed we lie upon, in the desire of my mind our bodies cling together although Ireland is between us. When my beloved sees how difficult it is for me he would not ask me to undertake a journey. May his part in the march across the old mead-plain of Munster not turn out like the journey of his brother, Hugh Maguire.'

Eochaidh seems to have had little to do with Cú Chonnacht after Kinsale, but there does not appear to have been a real breach. At any rate in a late poem to Brian Maguire, an appeal for help, Eochaidh points out how well he had been treated by his father and his two brothers. With the accession of James I, like many of the Irish, Eochaidh had a sudden access of hope. 'What a metamorphosis,' he says, 'Ovid should be alive. It would give him more to write about.' He lifts up his face to King James 'like a daisy to the sun.' But a cloud came over the sun and the whole subsequent impression of Eochaidh is one of despair and misery. Ireland was a land of interwoven tragedies and Eochaidh was involved in many of them. When he visited Rose O'Toole, the widow of O'Byrne, in Wicklow he made a suggestion of marriage, and this suggestion, perhaps half joking whole in earnest, is the only hint of a woman in Eochaidh's life. Rose, a figure worthy of Greek tragedy, had all the chieftain qualities that he admired. The O'Byrne poems are written in what we may call the period of the memory of the two Hughs. In one of these he writes: 'The two Hughs who have gone from me, my strength has gone with their power, like a bird that has lost the power of flight.' He is bitter also in a poem written in 1603 that facile metres now bring more praise than artistic metres, and he writes this poem in a facile metre to show that if being a dunce is a good thing he can excel even in this. 'I used to break my heart over my poems,' he tells us, 'but this type of verse is actually a cause of health to me.' His way of life was criticised. In a poem written to defend himself he says that he refuses to enter into a contest of reviling. He then tells the story of the woman taken in adultery with whom he implicitly identifies himself: if his critics are without sin let them cast the first stone. In another poem he claims the protection of God and with a strange mixture of pride and humility represents himself as 'a knee that never bowed to You before.'

What I regard as Eochaidh's last poem I would tentatively date to about 1610. At this time Eochaidh was about forty and the poem was written to a young man, Myles O'Reilly. Hugh Maguire is not mentioned explicitly but he appears in the character of the *triumvir* Marcus Crassus. In the nine years war Hugh was, in fact, an Irish *triumvir*, the other two being Red Hugh and Hugh O'Neill. Red Hugh appears in this poem as Pompey, Caesar is the English power, Eochaidh is Cornelia, who was first wife of Marcus Crassus (a slight distortion of Roman history here) and later of Pompey. The battle of Pharsalia is Kinsale. Although this is superficially a praise-poem it is, in fact, autobiographical. Myles was to die as a young man in 1617 and it would almost seem that Eochaidh had some idea that he was not to live long. Again I give a partial abstract:

'For love of him I shall abandon Myles. What harm is it to him if I do not give him my deepest love — I do not abandon him through lack of desire. I am cursed by a contrary fate: anyone who loves me dies. Where is the companion I loved, the trusted lord, that did not cause me woe? My cup is full; God has left me none of those who surrounded me. I have suffered through the O'Neills, the O'Donnells and the Maguires. Every prince, every heir to princedom, every companion I loved, all have gone and those who have not are in danger. Through love of him I cannot touch Myles: I love for spite and not for inclination. After all those, there would be danger that I might hasten Myles' death. Let Katharine's son give me no kind word, no affection, no wealth; let him forget his pleasure in my verse. Let him not raise his languid eye to me, let him give me no recognition. My counsel to him is to be hard

135

with me. Let my friend, my companion, make his
gentle face a thorn; else fate might ordain his death.
Since this is my curse I must never love him who is
the torment of the women of Ireland; it would be evil
of me to do so. I shall love none of the Irish; if I wish
their death I shall love the foreigner. When Pompey
came from battle his wife spoke as I am speaking.
There were two kings who divided the world, Pompey
and Caesar, and they quarrelled over the division. The
people of the world did battle in the Plain of Thessaly
and in that civil war the kings of the earth were slain.
Caesar was victorious and Pompey came dishonoured
from the battle. "Alas," said his wife, Cornelia, "that
your fortunes have changed and you are alone, great
king. The fault is mine, and but for me your power
would be upon the world. Marcus Crassus, my dear
first husband, one of the three pillars of the earth, I
brought him bad fortune. Your misfortune is from me.
Alas, that I did not marry Caesar.' So it is with me.
Like her I am to make a lover of those I hate: it will
not be my beloved of the descendants of Conn, since
he whom I love is not destined to live. He to whom I
wish evil, I have only to take him as a lover in order
to overthrow him. If I should give (as I have not given)
my deepest love to Myles may it not turn out for him
as for the warriors of Ulster. It is dangerous not to
believe in fate. If I do not love Myles it is not through
lack of desire. I am afraid that my heart will show him
the secret of my mind. Venus, the goddess of love,
may wound my mind with mad love for him. Seeking
to seduce me, she has shown me the bright expanse of
countenance, the modest gentle joyous face with
lovable fairy-like disposition. Perhaps his presents will

136

seduce me, his pleasant voice, his quiet mind, the majestic company of my youth . . .'

Eochaidh, like many other natives, received a grant of land in the Plantation of Ulster. But he obviously did not value land and property for itself: he wanted place, prestige, and dignity. He died on 2nd June, 1612 aged about 43.

One of the interesting things about Eochaidh's poetry is the conceit by which he represents himself as the lover or wife of the chief whom he is praising. This conceit may well have its roots in pre-Christian religion and institutions. The latest example known to me is in the seventeenth century poem already referred to, *Féuch féin an obair-se, a Aodh*. Eochaidh Ó hEoghusa represents the idea in the late sixteenth century and demands as a traditional right to be near the prince and to share his bed. In the fifteenth century a poet Lughaidh Ó Dálaigh goes to Trim to seek the grave of Féilim O'Reilly who has been slain there. As he looks at the grave he wishes to die too, and he recalls how things used to be: 'Let us be in the bed as we were before, O prince of Bóroimhe; we did not think a narrow bed too narrow for us two, O Féilim.' In a fourteenth century poem Seaán Ó Cluaáin addresses O'Connor whom he has hit with his fist and he appeals for a renewal of the friendship: 'O you of the fair hair, let us not be any longer without lying in the same bed, let us not be without drinking from the same cup. I am your lover, I am your bed companion, I am he who stands at your bright shoulder.'

In the coupling of the two ideas of the poet's being at the prince's shoulder, or side, and being his *fear éinleabtha* or bed companion Ó Cluaáin and Ó hEoghusa are clearly paraphrasing a traditional formula and this must be remembered in any judgment we make on the particular situation. The well-known poem *Géisidh cuan* is an eleventh century professional poem which was given a false saga setting and is thus a fossil preserved in the rock of *Acallam na Senórach*. Here the poet laments *an laech ro laiged lemm*, the warrior who used to lie with me. It could be maintained, but perhaps not with certainty, that one of the finest poems of this type is the ninth century poem in which the poet speaks in the character of the Old Woman of Beare. The poet, in such an interpretation, was what one may call a "king-lover": when old age was approaching he took unwillingly to religion: he expresses all his past experiences with kings in the person of an old harlot who after a good spring, summer, and autumn found herself rejected by her patrons in the early months of her winter. Another poem of this type is written by Guaire's poet, possibly the well-known Senchán. Guaire is good to him but his mind keeps straying towards Dínertach: 'These are the arrows that murder sleep at every hour in the cold night; desires (more do they come when day is gone) for the man from near the land of Roigne . . . I have everything from Guaire, the king of cold-peaked Aughty, but my mind strays from my people to the land in Irluachair.' This poem, like *Géisidh Cuan*, has been treated as a normal love-poem and given a demonstrably false saga-setting. It is the same theme and a similar treatment to what we find in the Costello-O'Rourke poem already mentioned.

There is one other matter to be referred to and I put it in the form of a question. We have followed especially the situation between Eochaidh and Hugh Maguire. What part did Gille Brighde Ó hEoghusa play in all this?   It certainly seems inescapable that he was involved in some way.

Gille Brighde was Eochaidh's brother or cousin and he was also a professional poet. Some poems are attributed in certain MSS to Eochaidh and in others to Gille Brighde. but it is usually possible to say whether Eochaidh wrote a particular poem or not. About 1603 Gille Brighde left Ireland and before leaving he wrote a poem to a close friend called Eoghan. In this poem he says that he is giving up his art for another, for book-learning. Eoghan is not to come with him: he will be better off amongst his own people. He, Gille Brighde, will never make another friend, and he counsels Eoghan to do as he does. Let them be like the turtle-dove, who when it loses its mate never takes another. He knows from his own feelings what anguish Eoghan must feel. Psychologically this is all very similar to Eochaidh. Gille Brighde crossed, it would appear, from Ireland to Wales on the first stage of the journey to the Low Countries. He was giving up his art, but since a poet cannot do this easily, he occupied the journey from Ireland to Wales by expressing his emotion in verse. But he was not thinking of Eoghan. He hates the sea because it hides the Irish mountains, and he hates the mountains on the other side because the sight of them means that he has lost Ireland. He counts his losses and they are not small. He has lost the land where he was reared from childhood and he may never see it again; he has lost his hereditary craft which he can practice no more. Then he makes the statement which brings him into this whole situation: 'Hugh Maguire, my darling, my beloved, my warrior, all losses were equal to me but the loss of you.'

This is no praise-poem, but a genuine confession of emotion and it is a tribute to the devotion which Hugh

could inspire. The solution that, of course, suggests itself
is that Gille Brighde was Eochaidh's *aithgin oile*, his 'own
like,' the man whose worthiness he conceded but of whom
he was jealous some years before. Gille Brighde was in
Douai in 1605 and in 1607 he entered the Franciscan
Convent in Louvain. He was ordained a priest in 1609.
He wrote an Irish grammar and in the few years that
remained, under the name of Bonaventura Ó hEoghusa, he
used his art in the cause of the counter-reformation. He
died a year after Eochaidh, and his death is the end of
that chapter in literary history that covers Eochaidh Ó
hEoghusa and his relationship to the Maguires of
Fermanagh.